Between the Lines

Enhancing Inferencing Skills

Cecile Cyrul Spector, PhD

Super Duper® Publications
Greenville, South Carolina

Between the Lines: Enhancing Inferencing Skills

Copyright © 2006 by Cecile Cyrul Spector. Cecile Cyrul Spector grants limited rights to individual professionals to reproduce and distribute pages that indicate duplication is permissible. Pages can be used for instruction only and must include Cecile Cyrul Spector's copyright notice. All rights are reserved for pages without the permission-to-reprint notice. No part of these pages can be reproduced in any form, electronic or mechanical, including photocopy, recording, or any information storage and retrieval system, without permission in writing from the publisher.

Made in the USA

Cover design by Sharon Webber

Cartoons by Paul Modjeski

Trademarks: All brand names and product names used in this book are tradenames, service marks, trademarks, or registered trademarks of their respective owners.

Super Duper® Publications
www.superduperinc.com
Post Office Box 24997 • Greenville, SC 29616 USA
1-800-277-8737 • Fax 1-800-7379

#TPX-29901   ISBN 978-1-58650-745-9

*For my much-loved brother Steven,
always in my heart and in my memory*

About the Author

Cecile Cyrul Spector has worked in the field of speech-language pathology for over 30 years. She received her BA and MA from Brooklyn College and her PhD from New York University. She started her career by providing clinical services in public schools, private practice, and at the Hofstra University clinic. Eventually she joined the faculty of Long Island University– Orangeburg Campus, where for 10 years she taught a wide range of courses and was the director of the speech-language department. She also taught many courses as an adjunct professor at Montclair State University and New York University.

Cecile has made numerous research presentations and given workshops that have focused on various aspects of humor, ambiguity, figurative language, and, more recently, inferencing. Most of her journal articles have been on this same subject matter.

As a clinician, Cecile has worked with individuals from 18 months to 80-plus years. Language-learning-disabled adolescents and adults who incurred brain injury as a result of strokes or accidents were the populations that sparked her interest in the subtleties of abstract language and cognition.

Family-oriented activities play a major role in Cecile's life. She also enjoys cooking, reading, hiking, swimming, playing her flute, and travel.

Cecile's previous publications include the following: *Just for Laughs* (Communication Skill Builders, a division of Harcourt Inc.); *Saying One Thing, Meaning Another; Sound Effects;* and *As Far As Words Go* (Thinking Publications).

Contents

Preface vii

Acknowledgments ix

Introduction

Overview 3

Goals 5

Target Populations 5

Rationale 6

The Development of Inferencing Skills 9

From Theory to Practice 11

Facilitator Techniques 12

Special Considerations 17

Assessing Inferencing Skills 17

Getting Started 20

Activity Sections

Section 1: Location Inferences 23

Section 2: Agent Inferences 31

Section 3: Time Inferences 39

Section 4: Action Inferences 47

Section 5: Instrument Inferences 55

Section 6: Category Inferences 63

Section 7: Object Inferences 71

Section 8: Feelings Inferences 79

Section 9: Cause and Effect Inferences 89

Section 10: Problem/Solution Inferences 99

Section 11: Proverbs 109

Contents

Section 12: Paragraph Analysis 121

Section 13: Visual Humor 127

Section 14: "Because" Statements 135

Section 15: Bridging Activities 143

Appendices

Appendix A: Location Warm-Ups 149

Appendix B: Agent Warm-Ups 153

Appendix C: Time Warm-Ups 157

Appendix D: Action Warm-Ups 160

Appendix E: Instrument Warm-Ups 164

Appendix F: Category Warm-Ups 169

Appendix G: Object Warm-Ups 176

Appendix H: Feelings Warm-Ups 178

Appendix I: Cause and Effect Warm-Ups 179

Appendix J: Problem/Solution Warm-Ups 181

Appendix K: Paragraph Analysis Story Webs 183

References 185

Preface

One day the captain caught the first mate drunk while on watch. The captain wrote in the ship's log, "The first mate was drunk on watch today." The first mate was very upset and begged the captain to remove the comment from the log. "After all, Captain, this was the first and only time it ever happened." "I only write the truth in this log," said the captain. The following day it was the first mate's turn to make entries in the ship's log. He wrote, "The captain was sober today."

If you can appreciate the amusing element in the last line of this joke, you can thank your inferencing skills. The need to infer crops up over and over again in our conversations, our literature, and in all aspects of the media. We are, in essence, "reading between the lines." This is challenging to our intellect. Our thought processes are stimulated, our background knowledge is scanned for a probable fit, and, at times, our sense of humor is tickled.

Some authors (e.g., Lazzari & Peters, 1988; Simon, 1993) have written intervention resources that include several activities for developing inferencing skills in older children, adolescents, and adults with language-based learning disabilities. However, resources that are devoted entirely to a wide range of inferencing skills are lacking.

In 2002 I conducted an informal study of the inferencing skills of 24 university undergraduate and graduate students for visual humor items (Spector, 2005). The students were asked to analyze a dozen cartoons and comic strips and infer the basis of the humor. The purpose of the study was to collect data from typically achieving individuals to provide a basis of comparison for individuals with impaired language abilities. I was surprised to find that even at that age (19 to 42 years) many typically developing individuals have gaps in their visual inferencing skills. If some members of this population could use a boost in their inferencing skills, imagine the need in individuals who, for example, have language-based learning disabilities, are hearing impaired, or have incurred trauma to the brain.

Through the years, I have used many of the activities included in *Between the Lines: Enhancing Inferencing Skills* in my intervention sessions. The results have been gratifying. The following comment was made by a reviewer who field tested this resource:

> Besides field testing it [*Between the Lines*] myself, I also shared some of the information and activities with the middle school ELL (English language learners) teacher and with a paraprofessional who works with one of my seventh grade students who has autism. These teachers also found the information to be very useful. As a result of reviewing and discussing the materials with them, they were better able to tap into this unique aspect of language development with their students. They were also able to provide me with

Preface

improved feedback on the students whom we share by giving me specific examples about students' inferential thinking in a variety of academic situations. (C. Ketter, personal communication, July 29, 2005)

For people who do not "read between the lines" a well-designed structure is needed to help them grasp inferences. *Between the Lines* provides such a structure for learning the innumerable inferences encountered in our daily lives. Inferences relating to time, space, actions, objects, feelings, cause and effect, and so forth, are explored in a step-by-step manner.

Acknowledgments

Once again, I am delighted to be working with all the very nice people at Thinking Publications. I shall always be grateful to Nancy McKinley for encouraging me to publish my first book. She was an amazing person and is sorely missed. Now, on book number four, I continue to enjoy my relationship with Thinking Publications. My thanks and gratitude to all those involved in the preparation of this book. In addition to smoothing out the rough edges of the original manuscript, my editor, Marietta Plummer, has been a source of truly creative suggestions throughout the editing process. It has been a pleasure working with her. Angie Sterling-Orth provided valuable input for improving *Between the Lines*. Her editing efforts made this a much better book than it would have been. My thanks also to Linda Schreiber and Jan Carroll for their part in the editing process. Many thanks to Dathan Boardman, who provided the book's graphic art. The cartoons in the visual humor section are the work of the very talented Paul Modjeski. It amazed me that he could take the ideas we discussed and depict them in such a delightful manner. Thank you, Paul.

I owe the reviewers of the original manuscript, Kathleen Gorman-Gard, Carla Ketter, Vicki Prouty, and Nola Radford, a debt of thanks. I hope I have made the best use of their insights, suggestions, and constructive criticisms.

My parents, Grace and Jack Cyrul, and my sister Glady, provided an environment that nurtured and encouraged my creative side. I hold them in loving memory. My wonderful family continues to provide encouragement and support of my writing efforts. Love and thanks to my husband, Mort, who acts as "consultant" during the preparation of my books. My daughter Lauren and her husband, Richard; my son, Jeffrey; my daughter Suzanne and her husband, Tom; and my grandchildren, David, Rachel, Sarah, and Stephanie, make my life rich and pleasurable. Their special talents and abilities give me the incentive to write books designed to help others be all that they can be. A special thank you to David for inspiring the "Because" section of this book.

Introduction

Introduction

Overview

Inferencing is a constant activity in our daily lives. For instance, if the blueberry bush in our backyard is stripped bare of berries, we infer that the birds have been feasting again. If a friend looks dejected after a job interview, we infer that she didn't get the job. We make these inferences by scanning our memory for matches between current and previous experiences and events. We use any clues available to support these inferences.

Between the Lines: Enhancing Inferencing Skills teaches individuals, age 9 through adult, to make appropriate inferences. The inference types in Sections 1–10 of *Between the Lines* are based on those set forth by Johnson and von Hoff Johnson (1986), researchers in the field of reading and cognition. Johnson and von Hoff Johnson examined the nature of the inferences found within textbooks. They listed the following major types of inferences students are likely to find in their textbooks:

- **Location** (deciding place from clues given)
  Example—Cathy put a towel over her wet bathing suit and brushed the sand off her feet before putting on her sandals. Where is Cathy?

- **Agent** (deciding occupation or role)
  Example—June had to order more roses and irises before she could arrange the flowers for the wedding bouquets and table centerpieces. What is June's occupation?

- **Time** (deciding when things occurred)
  Example—Ralph needed a flashlight to make his way from the tent to the outhouse. When did this occur?

- **Action** (deciding activity)
  Example—Shelby ran the bow over the strings to create a beautiful sound. What is Shelby doing?

- **Instrument** (deciding tool or device)
  Example—Just two or three more blows and the tree would fall. What tool was being used?

- **Category** (deciding class or group)
  Example—I love <u>Monopoly</u>, but my brother prefers <u>Checkers</u> or <u>Scrabble</u>. The underlined words are members of what category?

- **Object** (deciding item being talked about)
  Example—The cover and spine were in good condition, but many of the pages were dog-eared. What is being talked about?

- **Feelings** (deciding how someone may be feeling and why)
  Example—This was the first time Rowan's paintings were on exhibition at the art gallery. The gallery owner informed him that many people praised his work, and several of them asked if the paintings were for sale. What feeling(s) might Rowan be experiencing?

- **Cause and Effect** (deciding reason something happened or the outcome)
  Example—In the morning, we woke to find the trees stripped bare of their leaves and many broken branches strewn across the yard. What caused this to happen?

- **Problem/Solution** (deciding how to solve a problem)
  Example—Helene had an earache, but she was unable to reach her doctor. What should Helene do about this problem?

Between the Lines is organized in a hierarchical fashion. Sections 1–7 are less complex than sections 8–15. The contextual support (i.e., context clues, or key words and phrases) embedded in each item helps lead the individual to the appropriate inference. (An attempt was also made to arrange the items within each section in a hierarchical manner, from easy to difficult. This was not done, however, after a pilot study revealed a lack of consensus among subjects with regard to the difficulty level of each item.)

Sections 8–14 are more challenging, and they may require greater support from the facilitator. These sections involve inferences related to cause and effect, problem/solution, feelings, proverbs, paragraph analysis, visual humor, and "because" statements. These types of inferences require individuals to employ advanced levels of thinking skills (Bloom, Engelhart, Furst, Hill, & Krathwohl, 1956), that of analysis, synthesis, and evaluation. "Proverbs" is the only section that focuses solely on figurative language. Figurative language is often ambiguous, and understanding ambiguity requires the use of one's inferencing skills.

Sections 1–10 each include several Warm-Ups activities. Through the Warm-Ups the specific inferencing skill is taught. Following the Warm-Ups, several activity practice pages appear. The activity pages provide many opportunities for individuals to practice the specific type of inferencing. Sections 11–14 include Background Information and Let's Practice sections to introduce concepts before students complete those activity pages. Section 15 provides facilitators with ideas to bridge the information learned in *Between the Lines* into situations individuals will encounter at home or in school. This section combines a variety of inference types included in this resource.

At the end of each section, answer keys with suggested responses are provided for the items in the activity pages. However, individuals' responses will vary, and it is up to the facilitator to determine the appropriateness of any particular response. At times there may be several responses that are appropriate for an item. Comparing the answers given by individuals with those suggested for each item in the answer keys encourages thought-provoking discussions.

Between the Lines includes a variety of appendices to make more efficient use of the resource. An appendix is provided for each of the first 10 sections to include the reproducible materials needed for the Warm-Ups.

Goals

The primary goal of *Between the Lines* is to provide individuals with opportunities to improve their inferencing and other thinking skills (e.g., making predictions, solving problems, drawing conclusions), from the acquisition of knowledge through the evaluation of that knowledge. This can be done in one-on-one or group activities. Other semantic and pragmatic language goals can be achieved as well. The activities in this resource provide individuals with opportunities for:

- Enhancing their oral reasoning skills
- Analyzing and expressing feelings and behaviors
- Expanding utterances in discourse
- Enhancing world knowledge
- Enhancing vocabulary
- Developing creative responses
- Exploring humor in everyday activities and situations

Target Populations

The activities in *Between the Lines* are designed for older children (age 9 and above), adolescents, and adults, who:

- Have a language-based learning disability
- Have a reading disability
- Are English language learners
- Have incurred brain injury
- Are hearing impaired
- Have a mild form of autism or a related disability

- Possess typical learning and achievement but want to improve their understanding of subtle inferences in spoken and written language

Some individuals in the above-stated populations may find portions of the material in this book too difficult. It is incumbent upon the facilitator to determine whether the difficult material can be mastered with a greater amount of assistance, or whether to skip over those items entirely. Facilitator techniques for assisting individuals can be found on page 12.

Facilitators who might use this resource include speech-language pathologists, special education teachers, learning disabilities specialists, remedial reading specialists, general education teachers, and teachers of English language learners.

Rationale

So much of what we understand comes from our ability to infer meaning. That is, to guess, or surmise what is meant, by taking into account factors other than the words that make up the sentences in a statement, or the images in a picture. "We use prior experience and knowledge of the world for constructive comprehension. A discourse exchange is successful when the listener is able to fill in the details of a message" (Wallach & Miller, 1988, p. 115). "Reading between the lines" requires inferencing skills. Inferencing is a thinking skill. Thinking skill levels have been classified in a hierarchical fashion by Bloom et al. (1956). Starting with the most elemental and progressing to the most difficult, these levels are as follows:

- **Knowledge**—Individuals can recall bits of information.
- **Comprehension**—Individuals can understand information, but do not relate it to other material.
- **Application**—Individuals can use what is previously known to figure out problems under new circumstances.
- **Analysis**—Individuals can break a whole into its parts.
- **Synthesis**—Individuals can put parts together to create a new whole.
- **Evaluation**—Individuals can state opinions and give reasons; they can explain why; they can infer.

Evaluative thinking skills are at the highest level of the hierarchy and include the skill of inferencing. The ability to evaluate information encompasses the abilities that are requisite for all the previous thinking skill levels. There is no final stage to this sequence of thinking skills. Even when individuals reach the level of evaluation, the process of evaluating is likely to stimulate thinking in the previous levels and stimulate the cycle of learning through all the levels. There will be acquisition of new knowledge, new ways of comprehending or applying knowledge, and so forth. In a way, this illustrates the idea that the more we know, the more we become aware that there is yet more to know (i.e., *metacognition*—the voluntary, selective attention to one's own cognitive processes).

Researchers in numerous disciplines (such as speech-language pathology, remedial reading, teaching English language learners, general education, and teaching the hearing impaired) have investigated thinking skills (e.g., Baum, 1990; Bransford, Burns, Delclos, & Vye, 1986; Buehl, 2001; Cotton, 1988, 2001; Crump, Schlichter, & Palk, 1988; Gough, 1991; Haller, Child, & Walberg, 1988; Herrnstein, Nickerson, de Sanchez, & Swets, 1986; Johnson & von Hoff Johnson, 1986; Kagan, 1988; Laing & Kamhi, 2002; Spector, 1990; Wallach & Miller, 1988). Cotton (2001) provides a comprehensive review of research and resources for teaching thinking skills. She mentions numerous researchers (e.g., Baum; Cotton, 1988; Matthews, 1989; Sternberg & Bhana, 1986; Whimbey, 1985) who have examined a wide range of programs geared to improving thinking skills (e.g., verbal reasoning, problem solving, decision making, inferencing), including computer-assisted instruction. For example, Pogrow (1988) examined the *Higher Order Thinking Skills (HOTS)* program, and found it effective for the learning needs of at-risk students. Bass and Perkins (1984) investigated the effectiveness of computer-assisted instruction (CAI) to enhance the critical thinking skills of seventh grade students. For some thinking skills, Bass and Perkins found CAI to be effective; for others, conventional instruction proved to be better. It is important to note that *the appropriateness* of any particular intervention program for a targeted population *will determine its success* (Sternberg & Bhana). Inferencing was examined as one of many skills in these programs.

Making inferences is based on one's skill at actively making connections to one's store of background experiences and finding clues that help make these connections meaningful. Spector (1990) noted that adolescents with language-based learning disabilities had more difficulty making inferences regarding humorous and ambiguous utterances than their typically achieving peers. Pearson (1982) found that students with reading comprehension difficulties lacked skills such as drawing inferences, making predictions, and monitoring one's own understanding of written material. Myers's (1986) findings showed that individuals who have incurred traumatic brain injury have problems in many language areas, such as using contextual cues, understanding abstract language, and grasping inferred meaning. Doran and Anderson (2003) examined the inferencing skills of adolescent readers who are hearing impaired. They suggested that the difficulty these readers encounter when reading implicit material reflects the relative impoverishment of their experiential background. This also may be the case for some individuals in the other populations mentioned.

Between the Lines

Children, adolescents, and adults who have poor inferencing skills usually encounter a wide range of difficulties. They often misinterpret information, miss subtle cues, don't understand humor (e.g., jokes, riddles, comic strips, and cartoons), have difficulty interpreting what they read, have trouble understanding the feelings and motives of others, and so forth. When conversing, or reading, the individual must make connections between what is explicitly stated and what is implied. If a message is entirely explicit, there is no need for inferencing skills. However, this generally is not the case.

Fortunately, it is possible to enhance critical thinking abilities. Individuals who do poorly on tests that measure cognitive skills, such as inferencing, have been shown to improve considerably when given specific instruction and practice (e.g., Hudgins & Edelman, 1986; Kagan, 1988; Matthews, 1989; Pearson, 1982; Whimbey, 1985). State and national standards for educational institutions list inferencing as a required skill (Mid-Continent Research for Education and Learning, 2000). Inferential thinking is involved in standards such as: understands and applies basic principles of logic and reasoning; applies decision-making techniques; and applies basic problem-solving techniques. The materials in *Between the Lines* address these standards in many ways. For example, they enable the individual to:

- Identify problems and possible solutions
- Identify alternative courses of action and predict likely consequences of each
- Analyze and integrate contextual information
- Select the most appropriate strategy or alternative for solving a problem
- Select criteria or rules for category membership that are relevant and important
- Make contributions in group discussions (e.g., recount personal experiences; report on ideas and personal knowledge about a topic; connect ideas and experiences with those of others)
- Use inductive and deductive reasoning

Did You Know...

Separating inferred information from literal or given information is often difficult for both children and adults (Ackerman, 1986; Klein-Konigsberg, 1984).

Children as young as six can make inferences, but they become more capable of using inferential processing by seven or eight years of age (Westby, 1984).

Typically achieving children and children with learning disabilities have more difficulty answering inferential questions about stories than they do answering literal questions (Crais & Chapman, 1987).

= Introduction =

> Making inferences across sentences is more difficult than making inferences within sentences (Crais & Chapman).
>
> All types of inferences are made on an ongoing basis by using personal experience, background knowledge, and perception of activities in one's surroundings.
>
> Inferencing makes it possible for new, implicit, information to fit into our present mental schema. That is, "reading between the lines" is how we make sense of unstated information that has to be incorporated into what we already know.

The Development of Inferencing Skills

A wide range of language, learning, and thinking skills develop during the school years. It is fascinating to observe the acquisition and mastery of higher-order skills, such as inferencing, which rely on the development of both language and thought. Cognitive theories attempt to explain this development.

Cognitive Learning Theories

Cognitive learning theorists (e.g., Karmiloff-Smith, 1979; Piaget, 1985; Pinker, 1991; van Kleeck & Richardson, 1986; Vygotsky, 1962) offer differing explanations of how language behaviors are acquired. Focusing on the guiding principles of these theories enables professionals to effectively apply theory to language learning.

Cognitive learning theories focus on internal aspects of behavior and the individual's regulation of learning (Carrow-Woolfolk, 1988; Nelson, 1993; van Kleeck & Richardson, 1986). Klein and Moses (1994) organized cognitive learning theories into two categories they call *constructivist-cognitive* and *social-cognitive,* based on the theories' differing explanations of *how* language behaviors are acquired. For the purpose of this discussion, the Klein and Moses terminology will be used.

Constructivist-Cognitive

Supporters of constructivist-cognitive learning theories propose that the developmental aspects of language are not learned directly from others, but are modified as individuals interact with the environment in creative ways (Case, 1985; Fischer & Pipp, 1984; Karmiloff-Smith, 1979; Piaget, 1985; Pinker, 1991). Children's use of feedback from their own actions in the process of problem solving reflects the development of meaning. Thinking about their own language behavior makes children aware of these behaviors (Piaget). This awareness has been called *metalinguistic knowledge* (Kamhi, 1987; Karmiloff-Smith; Pinker, 1990; van Kleeck, 1984). Basically, at the core of a constructivist-cognitive view of language development is the individual's own creative activity.

From the constructivist-cognitive viewpoint, the focus is on developmental aspects of language, where abilities are acquired in a set order, and where certain abilities have to be acquired before others can emerge (Bloom & Lahey, 1978). Children engage in constructivist activities such as developing problem-solving procedures; reflecting upon actions and events in the environment; making inferences; and judging one's success or failure in achieving a language goal. Language emerges as a result of the child's constructive activity. However, it is the adult who creates a developmentally appropriate environment that allows for and stimulates constructive activity, helps to facilitate problem identification, and promotes the drawing of inferences.

Proponents of constructivist-cognitive theories believe that language learning is facilitated by the following:

- Interacting with materials and tasks commensurate with the individual's past experience, and present developmental level and interests
- Varying actions during problem solving
- Reflecting upon personal behavior and the environment
- Making inferences
- Using inductive and deductive reasoning

Social-Cognitive
The social-cognitive theories attempt to provide an explanation of how individuals learn language by focusing on information processing skills, how they acquire internal control over learning and problem solving, or, how they learn how to learn (Reid, 1988; van Kleeck & Richardson, 1986; Vygotsky, 1962). Pragmatic skills, the learning of conversational skills and knowledge about communication, are also examined. Social-cognitive learning theories differ from constructivist-cognitive theories in concluding that adults (and others) mediate children's development beyond only providing and designing the environment. Children acquire the features of language that are modeled by the adults in their lives (for example, internalizing verbal directions, or imitating problem-solving procedures). This learning also can be derived from children's peers as they interact at play, or participate in problem-solving activities (Nelson, 1993).

In essence, children observe, imitate, and internalize problem-solving procedures and other learning strategies demonstrated by others. They learn to use language internally to direct problem-solving procedures and to stop and redirect behavior. The adult directs the learner's attention to relevant stimuli in the environment.

Metacognition is the voluntary, selective attention to one's own cognitive processes. The social-cognitive learning theories focus upon metacognitive strategies for processing information. This involves strategies such as those needed for attending, organizing, remembering, inferencing, sequencing, and problem solving. The analysis and study of specific aspects of cognition as each is being performed are called *metaperception, metamemory*, and *metacommunication* or *metalinguistics* (Flavell & Wellman, 1980).

From Theory to Practice

Both constructivist-cognitive and social-cognitive learning theories provide us with many guiding principles for devising procedures to improve understanding of inferential language. For example, efforts to convey meaning successfully by repairing miscommunication of meaning is considered by proponents of both theories to be a principle of language learning. In addition, both constructivist- and social-cognitive theories recognize the need to consider a child's developmental level when planning intervention procedures. This important learning principle is found in Vygotsky's (1962) work. Vygotsky proposed that the influence of adults on language learning occurs within a zone of proximal development. This zone is that area between the child's developmental level as manifested in spontaneous behavior and the level the child can potentially achieve with adult guidance. Vygotsky views the child as developing and functioning within a social context. Social interaction is essential for the individual to develop.

Schneider and Watkins (1996) discuss the need for ongoing interaction which enables the individual to internalize strategies provided by the facilitator in joint problem-solving activities. The essential feature of this interaction is that facilitators adjust their assistance to the needs of the individual, retaining responsibility when the individual is less successful, and relinquishing it when the individual is doing well. The individual is learning the process of identifying the steps involved in an activity, not just how to perform any specific activity.

According to Lidz (1991), facilitators can mediate an experience in a dynamic interaction by:

- Helping the individual discriminate between what is important and what is not
- Helping the individual go from other- to self-regulation
- Mediating goal setting
- Mediating the level of difficulty of the activity so the individual can realize greater levels of competency without being overwhelmed

Social theorists stress naturalistic context as a strong determining factor in the acquisition of language structures. These theorists also recognize the need for language facilitators to adapt their input in response to the current needs of the individual with whom they are interacting, and to provide environmental experiences to assist individuals in expanding their world knowledge (i.e., use relevant content and contexts). Social theorists stress language function over language structure, as well as the importance of context.

Although the issue of assisting individuals who have lost language skills through injury to the brain, or individuals who are learning English as a second language, has not been addressed in this context, it seems reasonable that following the principles set forth in the constructivist-cognitive and social-cognitive theories would have a positive effect on their learning as well.

Facilitator Techniques

These general suggestions (adapted from Spector, 1997, 2002) may be helpful for promoting the active involvement of each individual when working on the various types of inferences. Providing appropriate support through facilitator techniques increases the likelihood that an individual will learn the inferencing skill.

Using Verbal Mediation

Offer ongoing verbal mediation, especially when presenting the Warm-Ups and examples. To elicit understanding from the individual it may be necessary to use verbal mediation to:

- Ask guiding questions that help reframe and refine the individual's contributions
- Supply information such as vocabulary definitions
- Provide some aspect of world knowledge
- Point out and discuss context clues

Even if the individual provides a correct response to an item, promote divergent thinking by asking further process-oriented questions such as:

- *How did you know which one to select?*
- *Why is that choice better than the others?*
- *What did you do to solve this question?*
- *Is there another way to look at the question?*

The facilitator also can ask for "bridging" information from the individual (Larson & McKinley, 2003; Wiig & Wiig, 1999). For example:

- *Can you think of another context in which you might use the same kind of thinking or the same strategy?*
- *Can you think of a time when you were in a similar situation?*

Fully discuss responses to the questions that follow each item so that a correct pattern of response is set. Continue to offer verbal mediation as long as necessary. Promote and facilitate ongoing discussions about the activity items. These discussions will provide opportunities for individuals to develop an awareness of visual and verbal cues that signal the need to make an inference, as well as opportunities to practice conversational interactions.

Brainstorming

Learning to infer is a form of problem solving. Brainstorming with individuals is one way of finding correct responses when items are missed. When brainstorming is used, acknowledge all responses given without making judgments regarding quality or correctness. This technique promotes the active involvement of each individual when working with a group. Encourage ongoing discussion about the items. For example, in the following situation a cause and effect relationship needs to be established.

Situation

Morty had just put the last book on the shelf, when suddenly it collapsed. What do you think could have caused this to happen?

Possible Brainstorming Comments Made by Facilitator and Students

- *It could be that Morty leaned too hard on the shelf.*
- *The bookshelf may have been made of inferior wood.*
- *The last book weighed a ton.*
- *Maybe there was an earthquake at just that moment.*
- *The weight of the books may have been too much for the shelf to hold.*
- *It was the straw that broke the camel's back.*

The facilitator should acknowledge that all of these are possibilities. Students should be asked which one seems to be the most likely choice and why. When appropriate, the facilitator should also expand upon comments made during brainstorming sessions. In this way, meaningful connections can be made between different aspects of language. For example, part of the last comment in the above brainstorming interaction ("the straw that broke the camel's back") can segue into a discussion of this well-known figurative expression.

Using Think Alouds

Have individuals "think aloud" when attempting to figure out potentially problematic items. This allows the individual to (1) consider alternate responses; (2) identify points of confusion; (3) point out and discuss context clues; (4) draw analogies to what is already known; and (5) use repair strategies when there is a failure to comprehend. Model this technique by saying things such as:

- *I need to figure out what* currants *are before I can decide in which category the word belongs.*

- *I think chalk dust can make someone sneeze. Who is often near chalk dust? I bet it's a teacher.*

- *I know that popcorn, candy, and soft drinks are sold in movie theatres. So probably the boys are sitting in a movie theatre.*

Looking for Context Clues

We interpret information in relation to the topic being discussed. Each item in the activities in *Between the Lines* has contextual support that can lead individuals to the correct interpretation of inferred material. Explain to students that we can often answer questions about statements that may seem puzzling at first by finding key words or phrases that give us clues. These clues are called *context clues*. Some items in *Between the Lines* have a great number of context clues; some items have clues that are quite subtle and difficult to ferret out. The level of help needed from the facilitator will vary from activity to activity and from item to item. The following is an example of an item with fairly obvious context clues.

Burt and Ernie were flopping around on the floor in a pool of water. Broken glass was all around them.

a. Who are Burt and Ernie? *(Burt and Ernie are probably goldfish.)*

b. What happened to them? *(They were in a fishbowl which was probably knocked over or dropped.)*

c. Which words or phrases give you clues? *(flopping around, pool of water, broken glass)*

Introduction

Explain to individuals that sometimes items have clues that are hard to find. They may be in the thought expressed by the item rather than in the words that the item comprises. Sometimes we must search our own experiences of a similar context in order to make a reasonable inference. The following is an example of an item that relies on our own experiences to help make an inference.

> The line at the supermarket was so long that Sylvia didn't know if she would be home in time to meet her children's school bus.
>
> a. How might Sylvia feel? *(worried, frustrated)*
>
> b. Which words or phrases give you clues to her feelings? *(The phrases "long line" and "didn't know if she would be home in time to meet her children's school bus" certainly give you clues, but using your own knowledge of how most people would feel in this type of situation is the strongest clue.)*

Discuss with individuals that while exploring the various types of inferences, context clues (in the form of key words or phrases) and background knowledge are available to help decipher the meaning that is implicit (hidden) in a statement. Help them see that finding the context clues becomes easier after they have more practice looking for them.

Explaining Unfamiliar Vocabulary

Individuals' performance can be adversely affected by their inability to understand some of the vocabulary in the activity items. Scan ahead in the targeted section for vocabulary that may be problematic. These words can then be discussed either before working on a particular section or as they occur. For example, in the following item the word *jodhpurs* is used.

> Katherine put on her jodhpurs and boots. The trail would be colorful on this beautiful autumn day. What was Katherine going to do?

Knowing the meaning of the word *jodhpurs* would provide an important clue for understanding this item. Unfamiliar vocabulary can be discussed in relation to its context clues (i.e., *boots* and *trail* relate to taking a trail ride on a horse). Encouraging the use of a level-appropriate dictionary to define unfamiliar vocabulary may also be beneficial during each section.

Assessing World Knowledge

Before beginning each section, review the items for aspects of world knowledge that, in your judgment, may be unknown to the individual. Discussing possibly unknown or sophisticated

Between the Lines

aspects of world knowledge would ensure better understanding of the items in *Between the Lines*. For example, in the following item, the term *aria* is used.

> Mario's voice was full and clear. Never had the aria sounded better. The audience applauded and shouted, "Bravo!"

A discussion of terms related to opera such as *aria* or *bravo* would provide information necessary for understanding the item. Or, for the following, knowledge of the words to the song "The Hokey Pokey" is required before the individual can infer the basis of the humor.

> The man who wrote "The Hokey Pokey" died peacefully at age 93. The most traumatic part for his family was getting him into the coffin. They put his left leg in. And then the trouble started.

If such discussions are not appropriate or helpful, skipping over or setting aside such items is recommended.

Exploring Visual Clues

For the items in the visual humor section, help individuals explore clues such as setting, situation, facial expressions, gestures, and body position of the cartoon characters. For example, in this comic strip item, the first frame shows a man standing on a scale wearing heavy boots.

"How do you expect me to weigh you while you're wearing those heavy boots?"

A nurse says, "How do you expect me to weigh you while you're wearing those heavy boots." In the second frame the man is holding the boots in his hands. If the man holds the boots while he is on the scale his weight will be the same as when he is wearing them. Noticing where the boots are in both frames allows one to infer the basis of the humor.

Using Referencing Texts

Make use of an idiom and proverb dictionary such as *The Concise Oxford Dictionary of Proverbs* (Simpson, 1996), *A Dictionary of American Idioms* (Makkai, Boatner, & Gates, 1995), or *NTC's American Idioms Dictionary* (Spears, 1996).

Special Considerations

Individuals from unique populations may have difficulties that require special attention when working on inferencing skills. For example:

- Individuals who have incurred brain injury may need items read several times because of impaired memory skills, or they may have difficulty responding because of impaired sensorimotor speech skills.

- Individuals with impaired hearing may need the support of sign language; emphasis on stress and intonation cues; or greater reliance on nonlinguistic cues such as facial expressions, gestures, body language, and so forth.

- Individuals who are English language learners or who come from linguistically diverse cultural backgrounds may need to have differences between the languages (or dialects) pointed out when inferring the meaning of an utterance. A word or phrase in one language may have a totally different meaning in another.

Assessing Inferencing Skills

If standardized scores are required (by a school district or other facility) to measure an individual's progress, the Test of Language Competence–Making Inferences subtest (TLC–E; Wiig & Secord, 1989) would be appropriate. The TLC–E has subtest and composite standard scores for students ages 5–9 (Level 1) and ages 10–18 (Level 2). Or, the various aspects of cognition, including inferencing, are measured by intelligence tests such as the Wechsler Intelligence Scale for Children–4th Edition (WISC–IV; Wechsler, 2003) or the Wechsler Adult Intelligence Scales–3rd Edition (WAIS–III; Wechsler, 1997). Scores for these tests may be available in school or psychological records.

Inferencing skills can be informally measured before and after an individual is exposed to the materials in *Between the Lines*. Select five items from the Informal Assessment section on pages 18–19 before teaching inferencing, and select five different items after teaching inferencing. Selection of the items should be random. Random selection of pre- and posttest items ensures a result that is more representative of the ability of the individual being tested (Edwards, 1973).

BETWEEN THE LINES

Informal Assessment

Select five of the following items before teaching inferencing and five different items after teaching inferencing. Read the desired items aloud. Ask students to write their answers on a separate sheet of paper.

1. When your mom is angry with your dad, don't let her brush your hair.
   a. What might happen? *(She will brush hard and hurt your head.)*
   b. Why would this happen? *(When people are angry, they sometime let their emotions out on others.)*
   c. Which key words give you clues? *(angry with your dad)*

2. Kortney brought hers to her friend's house for the sleepover. It would help make sleeping on the floor a little more comfortable.
   a. What is being talked about? *(a sleeping bag)*
   b. Which key words give you clues to the object being talked about? *(sleepover, sleeping on the floor a little more comfortable)*

3. Evan sneezed when his hair was being cut. It had to be cut even shorter.
   a. What caused this to happen? *(When he sneezed he moved his head, and his hair got cut unevenly. It had to be cut shorter to make it look even.)*
   b. Which key words give you clues to the cause? *(sneezed, when his hair was being cut)*
   c. How might this affect Evan? *(He might not like his hair so short, and he might feel embarrassed.)*

4. John waited impatiently at the red light. He was in a hurry to get to his friend's house.
   a. What was John doing? *(driving, walking, or biking to his friend's house)*
   b. Which key words give you clues to John's action? *(red light, was in a hurry to get to his friend's house)*

5. Kesia was asked by her boss to take care of his dog while he was on vacation. Kesia is afraid of dogs and doesn't feel comfortable with this task. She is afraid her boss will be upset if she declines the request.
   a. What is Kesia's problem? *(Her boss wants her to take care of his dog, but she doesn't want to.)*
   b. What could Kesia do? *(She could ask friends or coworkers if they would be interested in watching the dog. If she found someone else to watch the dog, her boss would probably be satisfied.)*

6. The Johnson family got checked in. They went to their room. The children couldn't wait to see the pool.
   a. Where were the Johnsons? *(at a hotel)*
   b. Which key words give you clues to the Johnson's location? *(checked in, room, pool)*

7. Linda arranged the roses in a vase. Then she added lilies and fresh greenery. She displayed the beautiful bouquet in the window.
   a. What is Linda's occupation? *(She's a florist.)*
   b. Which key words give you clues to Linda's occupation? *(arranged the roses, lilies, fresh greenery, bouquet)*

8. It was almost midnight. Soon the countdown would begin. At the stroke of midnight everyone would cheer and make a toast.
   a. When did this occur? *(New Year's Eve)*
   b. Which key words give you clues to the time? *(midnight, countdown, cheer, make a toast)*

9. A road full of puddles is not a good place for a child in new shoes to take a walk.
   a. What is likely to happen? *(The child would walk in the puddles and get the new shoes wet.)*
   b. Why would this happen? *(Children love to splash around in puddles.)*
   c. Which key words give you clues? *(puddles, child, new shoes)*

10. Scott hit "play." Then he listened to the message that was left for him.
    a. What device was Scott using? *(an answering machine)*
    b. Which key words give you clues to the device Scott was using? *(hit "play," listened to the message that was left for him)*

11. I love custard-filled, jelly-filled, and ones with sprinkles.
    a. What category do the underlined words belong to? *(doughnuts or sweet rolls)*

12. Never ask your three-year-old brother to hold a tomato.
    a. What might happen? *(He'll squeeze too hard and crush the tomato.)*
    b. Why would this happen? *(Young children don't know how to handle delicate things.)*
    c. Which key words give you clues? *(three-year-old, tomato)*

13. Jacob frowned when his teacher handed back his history test. He had studied all night, yet he only got a "C."
    a. What feeling(s) might Jacob have experienced? *(disappointment)*
    b. Which words give you a clue for why he may have felt this way? *(frowned, studied all night, "C")*
    c. Explain a time when you felt this way.

14. You can't trust a dog to watch your food.
    a. What would happen if you did? *(The dog would eat the food.)*
    b. Why would this happen? *(Dogs are known for eating whatever food they can get.)*
    c. Which key words give you clues? *(dog, watch, food)*

BETWEEN THE LINES

Getting Started

Before presenting the activities, review the following guidelines:

1. This book is arranged in a hierarchal manner. It is recommended that you begin with Section 1 and complete each section in order. Begin Sections 1–10 with the Warm-Ups provided. When engaging in the Follow-Up Discussions, encourage students to use their own background knowledge to successfully complete each activity page. Begin Sections 11–14 with the Let's Practice section to introduce the concepts before completing the activity pages.

2. Read aloud the examples at the beginning of each activity section, and work together to complete these items.

3. Copy the activity pages and distribute to each individual. When working with groups, consider making overhead transparencies to use during the activity rather than, or in addition to, using handouts.

4. Decide whether to read and complete the items together or to have the individuals read and complete them alone. This decision should be based on what would be beneficial for each individual. When possible, it is best for individuals to see each item as well as hear it read aloud.

5. Decide whether responses to stimulus items will be written or oral. Again, this decision should be based on what is best for each individual. The mode of presenting the items (on individual pages or on an overhead projector) also will affect this decision.

6. Use the facilitator techniques described on pages 12–15 to encourage ongoing discussion about the items in the practice and activity sections, and promote the active involvement of each individual when working with a group. Compare the answers given by each individual with those suggested in the answer keys to evoke further discussion.

Activity Sections

Section 1: Location Inferences 23
Section 2: Agent Inferences 31
Section 3: Time Inferences 39
Section 4: Action Inferences 47
Section 5: Instrument Inferences 55
Section 6: Category Inferences 63
Section 7: Object Inferences 71
Section 8: Feelings Inferences 79
Section 9: Cause and Effect Inferences 89
Section 10: Problem/Solution Inferences 99
Section 11: Proverbs 109
Section 12: Paragraph Analysis 121
Section 13: Visual Humor 127
Section 14: "Because" Statements 135
Section 15: Bridging Activities 143

Section 1: Location Inferences

Warm-Ups

Before using the activity pages in this section, use the following warm-ups to teach the concept of location inferences.

Hot and Cold

Play a variation of the game Hot or Cold where an individual must find a hidden object by having others in a group direct the search by saying, "You're hot!" if the searcher is nearing the hidden object, or, "You're cold!" if the searcher is getting farther away from the object. However, instead of "hot" or "cold," ask the group members to supply location hints without actually stating the location. For example, "It's on the other side of the room," "It's lower than the windowsill," "It's under a folder," and so forth. After the object is found, ask students which hints they thought were the most helpful to the searcher. Offering location information will improve with practice as students are taught to visualize surroundings to imply a location.

Make It Clear!

Provide each student with a highlighter and a copy of the *Make It Clear Statements* in Appendix A on page 149. Clues in these sentences explicitly state *where* something happens. This will draw specific attention to the concept of location. For example, consider this statement: *Amy was going to buy a new pair of shoes, so she tried on a pair at the mall.* It is clear that Amy is at a shoe store at the mall. Go through each situation listed on the *Make It Clear Statements* sheet and ask students to highlight the location that is clearly stated.

Location Guesstimation Crossword

Make a copy the *Location Guesstimation Crossword* in Appendix A on page 150 for each student. The clues for this crossword puzzle are sentences where the location is implied. Read each clue aloud, discussing the need to use the information in the sentence to discover the location. Then work together with students to fill in the correct responses. An answer key is provided on page 151.

Location Think Alouds

Copy the *Location Think Aloud Situations* in Appendix A on page 152. Use the Think Aloud technique explained on page 14 to model thoughts that wonder about and explain information. This technique enables one to predict; visualize; make personal and emotional responses clear; and reflect on a statement and its meaning. For example:

BETWEEN THE LINES

Situation

Joey wanted a peanut butter sandwich, so he opened the pantry and took out the jar of peanut butter. After he spread the peanut butter on the bread, he laid the knife on the counter.

Possible Think Alouds

I wonder where Joey is.

Where would you make a sandwich?

Where is the pantry.

Pantries are usually in or near the kitchen.

I think he's in the kitchen, because that's where food and knives are kept, and kitchens have counters.

Use the Think Aloud technique as the situations provided in Appendix A are discussed with students. Encourage students to add their own Think Alouds as they become more comfortable with this technique.

Follow-Up Discussion

Following the above activities, discuss that sometimes the location of a person or object is not always clear in conversation or when reading. However, by using context clues and prior knowledge, the location can be inferred. Remind students that they have now learned ways to infer a location. Explain that they will now have opportunities to practice this skill with the provided *Location Activity* pages.

Remember

Before using the activity pages in this section, scan the items to determine vocabulary or world knowledge that might be unfamiliar or confusing to students. Discuss these concepts before working on the inferencing activity pages. However, be careful not to inadvertently provide too much information, taking away from the individual's opportunity to figure out new word(s) or world knowledge independently.

Section 1: Location Inferences

NAME:_____ DATE:_____

Directions—Location Activity 1

For each item on this page, a location (place) is implied. Carefully examine each item for key words or phrases that will help you infer the location. Let's look at the example.

Example

Joe walked down the aisles quickly because the time on the parking meter was running out. Fortunately, he only needed bread, milk, and eggs.
  a. Where was Joe? *(at the supermarket, grocery store)*
  b. Which key words give you clues? *(aisles; bread, milk, and eggs)*

1 Sally shivered as she ran across the sand to get her towel.
  a. Where was Sally?
  b. Which key words give you clues to Sally's location?

2 The sound of all the crying newborn babies made Judy nervous.
  a. Where was Judy?
  b. Which key words give you clues to Judy's location?

3 Jeff's teammates cheered loudly when he hit a home run in the ninth inning. They ended up winning the game.
  a. Where was Jeff?
  b. Which key words give you clues to Jeff's location?

4 Carly was talking loudly when she was asked to be quiet. Other people were reading and trying to concentrate.
  a. Where was Carly?
  b. Which key words give you clues to Carly's location?

5 Alec ran across the field and kicked the ball as hard as he could, but the goalie was ready for it and prevented it from reaching the goal.
  a. Where was Alec?
  b. Which key words give you clues to Alec's location?

BETWEEN THE LINES

NAME:_____ DATE:_____

Directions—Location Activity 2

For each item on this page, a location (place) is implied. Carefully examine each item for key words or phrases that will help you infer the location.

1 Suzanne did several figure eights before she practiced her spins.

   a. Where was Suzanne?

   b. Which key words give you clues to Suzanne's location?

2 The rocking motion was making Stan sick. He couldn't wait to plant his feet on solid ground again.

   a. Where was Stan?

   b. Which key words give you clues to Stan's location?

3 The boys in front of Dillon kept jumping out of their seats to get popcorn, candy, and soft drinks. It was very annoying.

   a. Where was Dillon?

   b. Which key words give you clues to Dillon's location?

4 When Pavarotti sang the last aria, the audience applauded wildly and yelled, "Bravo!"

   a. Where was Pavarotti?

   b. Which key words give you clues to Pavarotti's location?

5 Lauren decided to chew gum on the way up and on the way down to keep her ears from popping.

   a. Where was Lauren?

   b. Which key words give you clues to Lauren's location?

6 After looking through all the brochures about Mexico, Marietta decided to go to Cancun. The travel agent offered her coffee before she got on the phone to make the hotel and airline reservations.

   a. Where was Marietta?

   b. Which key words give you clues to Marietta's location?

Section 1: Location Inferences

NAME:_____ DATE:_____

Directions—Location Activity 3

For each item on this page, a location (place) is implied. Carefully examine each item for key words or phrases that will help you infer the location.

1 Lian decided to have her hair restyled. She was very unhappy when she looked in the mirror and saw how short her hair was cut.

    a. Where was Lian?

    b. Which key words give you clues to Lian's location?

2 Tom picked three trees, six shrubs, and assorted flowering plants for his landscaping project.

    a. Where was Tom?

    b. Which key words give you clues to Tom's location?

3 Alfie and his friends took a walk along 42nd Street. They decided to have dinner at a restaurant near the Empire State Building before going to a Broadway show.

    a. Where were Alfie and his friends?

    b. Which key words give you clues to Alfie and his friend's location?

4 Rod had to take down the mainsail because the wind was too strong. He hoped to make shore before the weather got any worse.

    a. Where was Rod?

    b. Which key words give you clues to Rod's location?

5 The eggs were collected and the cows were milked. Now Chloe could go in and prepare breakfast for the family.

    a. Where was Chloe?

    b. Which key words give you clues to Chloe's location?

6 Angel ordered a cheeseburger. He also ordered fries and a soft drink.

    a. Where was Angel?

    b. Which key words give you clues to Angel's location?

BETWEEN THE LINES

NAME:_____   DATE:_____

Directions—Location Activity 4

For each item on this page, a location (place) is implied. Carefully examine each item for key words or phrases that will help you infer the location.

1. The orchestra's warm-up session was almost over. The actors waited nervously in the wings. The audience was anxious for the show to start.

   a. Where was the audience?

   b. Which key words give you clues to the audience's location?

2. Kate graciously accepted the Oscar for best actress and made a short speech. She looked lovely in her buttercup yellow gown.

   a. Where was Kate?

   b. Which key words give you clues to Kate's location?

3. The snow fell all night, and the trails were pristine. Eduardo rushed to the lifts so he could be the first one down.

   a. Where was Eduardo?

   b. Which key words give you clues to Eduardo's location?

4. "The chart seemed easier to read last year," thought Chue. He was afraid his vision was getting worse and that he would need stronger glasses.

   a. Where was Chue?

   b. Which key words give you clues to Chue's location?

5. Justin paid five dollars for the bag. He was told he could pick as many apples as the bag could hold.

   a. Where was Justin?

   b. Which key words give you clues to Justin's location?

6. The clowns came running in just as the acrobats finished their high-wire act. Rita noticed that the tent was filled to capacity.

   a. Where was Rita?

   b. Which key words give you clues to Rita's location?

Section 1: Location Inferences

Answer Key

These answers are merely suggestions. The facilitator should judge if the individual's responses are appropriate for each item.

Location Activity 1 (page 25)

1. a. at the beach
   b. shivered, sand, towel

2. a. at the hospital, maternity ward
   b. crying newborn babies

3. a. in a ballpark
   b. teammates cheered, hit a home run, ninth inning

4. a. at the library
   b. asked to be quiet, people were reading, trying to concentrate

5. a. on the soccer field
   b. ran across the field, kicked the ball, the goalie, goal

Location Activity 2 (page 26)

1. a. at a skating rink
   b. figure eights, practiced her spins

2. a. on a boat or ship
   b. rocking motion, sick, plant his feet on solid ground again

3. a. at a movie theater or sporting event
   b. boys in front; jumping out of their seats; popcorn, candy, and soft drinks

4. a. on the stage at an opera house
   b. Pavarotti; aria; audience applauded; yelled, "Bravo!"

5. a. on an airplane or elevator
   b. chew gum; on the way up and on the way down; keep her ears from popping

6. a. at a travel agency
   b. brochures about Mexico; decided to go to Cancun; travel agent offered her coffee; make the hotel and airline reservations

BETWEEN THE LINES

Location Activity 3 (page 27)

1. a. at a beauty salon
   b. hair restyled, saw how short her hair was cut

2. a. at a plant nursery
   b. trees, shrubs, flowering plants, landscaping

3. a. in New York City
   b. 42nd Street, Empire State Building, Broadway show

4. a. on a sailboat
   b. mainsail, make shore

5. a. on a farm
   b. eggs were collected, cows were milked

6. a. at a fast food restaurant (McDonald's, Burger King)
   b. cheeseburger, fries, soft drink

Location Activity 4 (page 28)

1. a. at a theater or auditorium
   b. orchestra, actors waited nervously in the wings, audience, show

2. a. at the Academy Awards
   b. Oscar for best actress, short speech, gown

3. a. at a ski resort
   b. snow, trails, lifts, first one down

4. a. at the ophthalmologist's (oculist's, or optometrist's) office
   b. chart, easier to read, vision, need stronger glasses

5. a. at an apple orchard
   b. paid five dollars for the bag, pick, apples

6. a. at the circus
   b. clowns, acrobats, high wire-act, tent

Section 2: Agent Inferences

Warm-Ups

Before using the activity pages in this section, use the following warm-ups to teach the concept of agent (occupation) inferences.

What Am I?

Copy and cut apart the *What Am I?* cards in Appendix B on pages 153–154. Each card provides three clues about a person's occupation. Divide students into two teams. Select a card and read the first clue to Team A, asking them to attempt to guess the occupation. If they guess correctly, Team A receives 3 points; if they do not guess correctly, read the next clue. If they guess with the second clue, the team will receive 2 points; if they need all three clues they only receive 1 point. For example:

> I sit on a very tall chair.—3 points
> I have to keep my eyes on the water.—2 points
> I make sure no one will drown.—1 point *(a lifeguard)*

Continue play as time allows, alternating turns between teams. While playing, have students discuss how they were able to determine the occupation (e.g., *A lifeguard sits on a tall chair so he or she can easily see the people in the water. Lifeguards prevent people from drowning*).

Occupation Highlights

Make a copy of the *Occupation Highlights* in Appendix B on page 155 for each student. Provide each student with a highlighter and an *Occupation Highlights* page. Have students highlight the statement(s) that would be true for each occupation. For example:

> A teacher:
> a. Is likely to have a desk covered with books and papers
> b. Goes to Paris for three weeks every year in October
> c. Spends many evenings grading papers

(It would be correct to highlight *a* and *c*.)

Follow-Up Discussion

Following the above activities, discuss that sometimes a person's occupation title or role is not stated during a conversation or in a reading. However, by using context clues and prior knowledge about various occupations, the agent can be inferred. Remind students that they have now learned ways to infer an agent. Explain that they will now have opportunities to practice this skill with the provided *Agent Activity* pages.

BETWEEN THE LINES

Remember

Before using the activity pages in this section, scan the items to determine vocabulary or world knowledge that might be unfamiliar or confusing to students. Discuss these concepts before working on the inferencing activity pages. However, be careful not to inadvertently provide too much information, taking away from the individual's opportunity to figure out new word(s) or world knowledge independently.

Section 2: Agent Inferences

NAME:_____ DATE:_____

| Directions—Agent Activity 1 |

For each item on this page, a person's occupation or role is implied. Carefully examine each item for key words or phrases that will help you infer the agent. Let's look at the example.

Example

Sidney scrapped the scales and filleted the fish. He had three more fish to clean.
- a. What does Sidney do? *(he works at a fish market)*
- b. Which key words give you clues to Sidney's occupation? *(scrapped the scales, filleted the fish)*

---

1 Beverly used her throat spray before practicing the scales. The lead role was very demanding and put great strain on her voice.
- a. What is Beverly's job?
- b. Which key words give you clues to Beverly's occupation?

2 Annette looked at the stack of tests in front of her. She wanted them all corrected to hand back to the students tomorrow.
- a. What is Annette's job?
- b. Which key words give you clues to Annette's occupation?

3 The treasure was supposed to be near the coral reef. Unfortunately, Bill had used up most of the air in his tank, so he would have to continue to search the water another time.
- a. What is Bill's job?
- b. Which key words give you clues to Bill's occupation?

4 The clouds were thick, and visibility was poor. Andrew wouldn't be able to relax until he landed the plane.
- a. What is Andrew's job?
- b. Which key words give you clues to Andrew's occupation?

5 Roy held his whip and spoke gently but firmly to the large cats. They obeyed his command to jump through the large hoop.
- a. What is Roy's job?
- b. Which key words give you clues to Roy's occupation?

Between the Lines © 2006 C.C. Spector. Published by Thinking Publications.
Duplication permitted for educational use only.

BETWEEN THE LINES

NAME:_____ DATE:_____

Directions—Agent Activity 2

For each item on this page, a person's occupation or role is implied. Carefully examine each item for key words or phrases that will help you infer the agent.

1 The article Grace was preparing for the school paper was too long, but she managed to remove the excess words in time to make her deadline.
  a. What is Grace's job?
  b. Which key words give you clues to Grace's role?

2 Ted told the passenger she had to pay a fare for her seven-year-old son. Only children six or under ride free. She put the money in the coin box and walked toward the back seats.
  a. What is Ted's job?
  b. Which key words give you clues to Ted's occupation?

3 After Bernadette took their order, she asked the busboy to bring water and a basket of hot rolls to their table.
  a. What is Bernadette's job?
  b. Which key words give you clues to Bernadette's occupation?

4 Madonna never sounded better. Her audience's thunderous applause filled the hall.
  a. What is Madonna's job?
  b. Which key words give you clues to Madonna's occupation?

5 As the visitors walked through the museum, Whitney pointed out and discussed the most famous of the paintings. She had done this tour so many times she knew her talk by heart.
  a. What is Whitney's job?
  b. Which key words give you clues to Whitney's occupation?

6 Angie read the chapter again and made two more corrections. She suggested one change to improve the last paragraph. At this rate, the manuscript would be ready for publication in the fall.
  a. What is Angie's job?
  b. Which key words give you clues to Angie's occupation?

Section 2: Agent Inferences

NAME:_____ DATE:_____

Directions—Agent Activity 3

For each item on this page, a person's occupation or role is implied. Carefully examine each item for key words or phrases that will help you infer the agent.

1 Richard worked on the brief all evening because he had to appear in court the next day.
   a. What is Richard's job?
   b. Which key words give you clues to Richard's occupation?

2 This was the third time this week Tim was called in the middle of the night. He was tired, but this was a small thing compared to the thrill of bringing a new life into the world.
   a. What is Tim's job?
   b. Which key words give you clues to Tim's occupation?

3 Mercedes put down the clippers and file. She looked through the bottles of polish and finally found a shade to Mrs. Roger's liking.
   a. What is Mercedes' job?
   b. Which key words give you clues to Mercedes' occupation?

4 Walter showed seven couples around the lot before lunch. All the couples wanted to see the latest models. Three of the couples wanted to go for a test drive.
   a. What is Walter's job?
   b. Which key words give you clues to Walter's occupation?

5 Stan applied heat and then massaged Marylou's ankle. He led her through a series of exercises that would help strengthen the healing bone.
   a. What is Stan's job?
   b. Which key words give you clues to Stan's occupation?

6 The examination took about 20 minutes. Dr. Max said the new lens would fit into the old frames and would be ready in a day or two.
   a. What is Dr. Max's job?
   b. Which key words give you clues?

BETWEEN THE LINES

NAME:_____ DATE:_____

Directions—Agent Activity 4

For each item on this page, a person's occupation or role is implied. Carefully examine each item for key words or phrases that will help you infer the agent.

1. After filling the detergent and bleach dispensing machine, Ernie checked the dryers to see if they were all emptied.
   a. What is Ernie's job?
   b. Which key words give you clues to Ernie's occupation?

2. Yesterday Sam's forecast was absolutely on the mark. He hoped he would have as much luck predicting temperature and humidity changes in the future.
   a. What is Sam's job?
   b. Which key words give you clues to Sam's occupation?

3. Xavier put the finishing touches on the wedding cake. Now it was time to prepare the dough for the cookies that had to be ready by 3 o'clock.
   a. What is Xavier's job?
   b. Which key words give you clues to Xavier's occupation?

4. The stains on the carpeting were not coming out, so Charlie used a stronger solution. Now that the Blakes had a new puppy, his job had become more difficult.
   a. What is Charlie's job?
   b. Which key words give you clues to Charlie's occupation?

5. The girls on the team finished the warm-up exercises early, so Norma told them to run around the track for a few minutes. The other team was not expected for at least a half hour.
   a. What is Norma's job?
   b. Which key words give you clues to Norma's occupation?

6. The room was fairly large. After measuring the walls, Malik ordered twelve double rolls. People often recommended him to their friends because he was a careful worker, and the seams always matched perfectly.
   a. What is Malik's job?
   b. Which key words give you clues to Malik's occupation?

Section 2: Agent Inferences

Answer Key

These answers are merely suggestions. The facilitator should judge if the individual's responses are appropriate for each item.

Agent Activity 1 (page 33)

1. a. She is a singer.
   b. used her throat spray, practicing the scales, lead role, great strain on her voice

2. a. She's a teacher.
   b. tests, corrected, hand back to the students

3. a. He's a deep-sea diver (scuba diver).
   b. treasure, near the coral reef, used up most of the air in his tank, search the water

4. a. He's a pilot.
   b. visibility was poor, wouldn't be able to relax until he landed the plane

5. a. He's an animal trainer.
   b. whip, large cats, command to jump through the large hoop

Agent Activity 2 (page 34)

1. a. She's a writer or journalist.
   b. article, school paper, remove the excess words, make her deadline

2. a. He drives a bus.
   b. passenger, pay a fare, put money in the coin box, back seats

3. a. She's a waitress.
   b. took their order, busboy, bring water and a basket of hot rolls

4. a. She is a singer.
   b. Madonna, never sounded better, audience, applause, hall

5. a. She's a docent (museum/tour guide).
   b. museum; pointed out and discussed; paintings; tour

6. a. She's an editor.
   b. read the chapter again, made two more corrections, suggested one change to improve the last paragraph, manuscript, ready for publication

BETWEEN THE LINES

Agent Activity 3 (page 35)

1. a. He's a lawyer (attorney).
   b. worked on the brief, appear in court

2. a. He's an obstetrician.
   b. called in the middle of the night, bringing a new life into the world

3. a. She's a manicurist.
   b. clippers and file; bottles of polish

4. a. He's a car salesman.
   b. the lot, latest models, a test drive

5. a. He's a physical therapist.
   b. applied heat, massaged Marylou's ankle, led her through a series of exercises, help strengthen the healing bone

6. a. He's an optometrist (eye doctor).
   b. examination, Dr., new lens, frames

Agent Activity 4 (page 36)

1. a. He's an attendant or owner of a laundromat.
   b. filling the detergent and bleach dispensing machine; checked the dryers

2. a. He's a meteorologist.
   b. forecast; predicting temperature and humidity changes

3. a. He's a baker.
   b. finishing touches on the wedding cake, prepare the dough for the cookies

4. a. He's a carpet cleaner.
   b. stains on the carpeting, used a stronger solution, new puppy, job had become more difficult

5. a. She's a coach.
   b. team, warm-up exercises, run around the track, other team

6. a. He's a wallpaperer.
   b. measuring the walls, ordered twelve double rolls, seams always matched perfectly

Section 3: Time Inferences

Warm-Ups

Before using the activity pages in this section, use the following warm-ups to teach the concept of time inferences.

Brainstorming

Use brainstorming to raise awareness of terms related to time (when something happens). Say to students, "Let's see how many words we can think of that relate to time, such as *morning, evening, early, before, after, dawn, dusk, yesterday, winter, summer, Halloween, Thanksgiving,* and so forth." Make a list of all the terms suggested and suggest other terms to add. Discuss the fact that time can refer to a specific time of day, seasons, holidays, the calendar, and when things happens in relation to each other (like *before* and *after*). Have students practice using the time terms in complete sentences.

Beat the Clock

Copy and cut apart the *Beat the Clock* cards in Appendix C on pages 157–158. Write the following time categories on the board for all students to see: Holidays, Seasons, Days of the Week, Months. Choose a card and tell students that they need to ask *yes/no* questions to try to figure out the time term on the card. Tell students the term belongs to one of the four categories. For example:

Student	**Facilitator**
Is it a month?	No
Is it a season?	Yes
Is it a hot season?	No
Is it a cold season?	Yes
Is it winter?	Yes!

Give each student 30 seconds to ask *yes/no* questions to try to guess the word. After the word is guessed or revealed, have the students tell in which category it belongs.

Name That Time

Make a copy of the *Name That Time* statements in Appendix C on page 159. These statements require a time inference. Read each statement aloud and ask students to tell when something occurred. For example: Marsha showered, dressed, and then prepared breakfast *(morning)*.

BETWEEN THE LINES

Follow-Up Discussion

Following the above activities, discuss that sometimes in a conversation or in writing the time an event occurs is not directly stated. However, with the use of context clues and background knowledge of time, when an event takes place can be inferred. Remind students that they have now learned ways to infer a time. Explain that they will now have opportunities to practice this skill with the provided *Time Activity* pages.

Remember

Before using the activity pages in this section, scan the items to determine vocabulary or world knowledge that might be unfamiliar or confusing to students. Discuss these concepts before working on the inferencing activity pages. However, be careful not to inadvertently provide too much information, taking away from the individual's opportunity to figure out new word(s) or world knowledge independently.

Section 3: Time Inferences

NAME:_____ DATE:_____

Directions—Time Activity 1

For each item on this page, the time something occurs is implied. Carefully examine each item for key words or phrases that will help you infer the time of the event. Let's look at the example.

Example

Jack took out the telescope and tried to see the rings of Saturn.
  a. When did this occur? *(in the evening, when stars and planets can be seen)*
  b. Which key words give you clues to the time? *(telescope, tried to see the rings of Saturn)*

---

1 Dorothy made coffee, scrambled the eggs, and fried the bacon. She put cereal bowls on the table for the younger children.
  a. When did this occur?
  b. Which key words give you clues to the time?

2 Harry was glad he was at the 18th hole. It was getting difficult to see the ball, and although it was summer, the air had become chilly.
  a. When did this occur?
  b. Which key words give you clues to the time?

3 Natalie was exhausted and did not look forward to driving home in the rush-hour traffic.
  a. When did this occur?
  b. Which key words give you clues to the time?

4 Dathan sleepily brushed his teeth and then set the alarm clock.
  a. When did this occur?
  b. Which key words give you clues to the time?

5 Jan was so excited. Now that summer was over, she would carry her new lunchbox, and get on the bus with all the other kids.
  a. When did this occur?
  b. Which key words give you clues to the time?

Between the Lines © 2006 C.C. Spector. Published by Thinking Publications.
Duplication permitted for educational use only.

BETWEEN THE LINES

NAME:_____ DATE:_____

Directions—Time Activity 2

For each item on this page, the time something occurs is implied. Carefully examine each item for key words or phrases that will help you infer the time of the event.

1 The crickets chirped, and the fireflies marked the sky with their intermittent glow.

  a. When did this occur?

  b. Which key words give you clues to the time?

2 Sarah had two sharp number two pencils. She had studied for hours the night before. She was nervous, but she was ready.

  a. When did this occur?

  b. Which key words give you clues to the time?

3 Paul was feeling relieved. The week had been so hectic, he was glad to be leaving school for the next two days.

  a. When did this occur?

  b. Which key words give you clues to the time?

4 Stephanie was so proud. This was the first time she ever skated at an outdoor rink, and she didn't fall on the ice even once!

  a. When did this occur?

  b. Which key words give you clues to the time?

5 Tony lit the candles on Lena's cake as everyone jumped up and yelled, "Surprise!"

  a. When did this occur?

  b. Which key words give you clues to the time?

6 Vicky brought souvenirs to the office for all of her co-workers. She had had a great time, but she was glad to be back.

  a. When did this occur?

  b. Which key words give you clues to the time?

Section 3: Time Inferences

NAME:_____ DATE:_____

| Directions—Time Activity 3 |

For each item on this page, the time something occurs is implied. Carefully examine each item for key words or phrases that will help you infer the time of the event.

1. At the lake, Elizabeth finally learned to do a backward flip off the diving board.
    a. When did this occur?
    b. Which key words give you clues to the time?

2. Tyler saved his sister a seat. They liked to sit far back when the film was widescreen.
    a. When did this occur?
    b. Which key words give you clues to the time?

3. Jimmy rowed the boat as fast as he could. He didn't realize how cold it could get on the river, and he didn't even have a pair of gloves.
    a. When did this occur?
    b. Which key words give you clues to the time?

4. Lorraine was exhausted, but she finally finished all the preparations for the party. Now she could get a good night's sleep.
    a. When did this occur?
    b. Which key words give you clues to the time?

5. The children could hardly wait. Their sparklers had all been used. The fireworks would be starting any minute.
    a. When did this occur?
    b. Which key words give you clues to the time?

6. It was the third time Celeste asked Michael if he was sure he had locked the doors and windows, and if he had the plane tickets. Celeste was so excited she couldn't stop talking.
    a. When did this occur?
    b. Which key words give you clues to the time?

Between the Lines © 2006 C.C. Spector. Published by Thinking Publications.
Duplication permitted for educational use only.

BETWEEN THE LINES

NAME:_____ DATE:_____

Directions—Time Activity 4

For each item on this page, the time something occurs is implied. Carefully examine each item for key words or phrases that will help you infer the time of the event.

1. The apple and pumpkin pies were sitting on the kitchen table. Robert kept checking the turkey. It was taking longer to roast than he thought, and the dressing, cranberry sauce, mashed potatoes, and vegetables were all ready. Robert had much to be thankful for this year.

    a. When did this occur?

    b. Which key words give you clues to the time?

2. Sally took off her shoes and rubbed her aching feet. She hadn't danced so much in a long time. It was so much fun!

    a. When did this occur?

    b. Which key words give you clues to the time?

3. The second bell was ringing just as Kelly tiptoed into class. Unfortunately, her mom had had a flat tire that needed to be repaired.

    a. When did this occur?

    b. Which key words give you clues to the time?

4. Grady rolled down the awning over the patio. The sun was very strong.

    a. When did this occur?

    b. Which key words give you clues to the time?

5. Randy turned on the porch light so his guests wouldn't trip in the dark.

    a. When did this occur?

    b. Which key words give you clues to the time?

6. The sun was in Marilyn's eyes as she ran to catch her bus. If she was late again she might get fired.

    a. When did this occur?

    b. Which key words give you clues to the time?

Section 3: Time Inferences

Answer Key

These answers are merely suggestions. The facilitator should judge if the individual's responses are appropriate for each item.

Time Activity 1 (page 41)

1. a. in the morning, time for breakfast
   b. coffee, scrambled the eggs, and fried the bacon; cereal bowls

2. a. at dusk, sunset, before a storm
   b. 18th hole, difficult to see the ball, air had become chilly

3. a. late afternoon, early evening
   b. exhausted, driving home, rush-hour traffic

4. a. bedtime
   b. sleepily brushed his teeth, set the alarm clock

5. a. first day of school
   b. summer was over, new lunchbox, get on the bus with the other kids

Time Activity 2 (page 42)

1. a. a summer evening
   b. crickets chirped, fireflies

2. a. before a test
   b. two sharp number two pencils, studied for hours the night before, nervous, ready

3. a. friday afternoon/early evening
   b. week, leaving school for the next two days

4. a. wintertime
   b. skated at an outdoor rink, ice

5. a. on Lena's birthday
   b. lit the candles on Lena's cake; yelled, "Surprise!"

6. a. after a vacation
   b. souvenirs, had a great time, was glad to be back

BETWEEN THE LINES

Time Activity 3 (page 43)

1. a. summertime
   b. at the lake, backward flip off the diving board

2. a. before a movie
   b. saved his sister a seat, film was widescreen

3. a. in the fall or early spring
   b. didn't realize how cold it could get on the river, didn't even have a pair of gloves

4. a. in the evening, before bedtime
   b. was exhausted, finally finished all the preparations, could get a good night's sleep

5. a. Independence Day
   b. sparklers, fireworks

6. a. on the way to the airport, before a trip
   b. asked; had locked the doors and windows; had the plane tickets; so excited

Time Activity 4 (page 44)

1. a. before Thanksgiving dinner
   b. apple and pumpkin pies; turkey; roast; dressing, cranberry sauce, mashed potatoes, and vegetables; to be thankful

2. a. after a dance or a party
   b. took off her shoes and rubbed her aching feet; hadn't danced so much; so much fun

3. a. at the beginning of the school day
   b. second bell was ringing, tiptoed into class

4. a. summertime, midday
   b. rolled down the awning over the patio, sun was very strong

5. a. in the evening, nighttime
   b. turned on the porch light

6. a. in the morning, before work
   b. sun, catch her bus, late again, get fired

Section 4: Action Inferences

Warm-Ups

Before using the activity pages in this section, use the following warm-ups to teach the concept of action inferences.

Gestures

Copy and cut apart the *Gestures* activity cards in Appendix D on pages 160–161. Have students take turns using gestures to illustrate an activity from one of the cards. Tell the others to guess (infer) what activity is being shown. For example, making the motions a pitcher would use when pitching to a batter, or, making the motions someone would use when taking a flag down from a flagpole. If there are a sufficient number of individuals, set up teams for a friendly competition in a charades fashion. Continue play as time allows, alternating between teams. While playing, have students discuss how they were able to determine the actions (e.g., "The way she was standing, looking down and reaching her arms out made it look like she was golfing"). This activity makes individuals aware of all the personal background knowledge they have stored in their memory that enables them to infer activities.

What Am I Doing?

Copy and cut apart the *What Am I Doing?* cards in Appendix D on pages 162–163. Each card provides four clues about a person's activity. Divide students into two teams. Select a card and read the first clue on the card to Team A, asking them to attempt to guess the activity. If they guess correctly, Team A receives 4 points; if they do not guess correctly, read the next clue for 3 points. If they do not guess correctly, read the next clue for 2 points. If they need all four clues, they only receive 1 point. For example:

Helen turned on the oven.—4 points
She beat the eggs and oil.—3 points
She added flour, baking powder, sugar, and salt to the bowl.—2 points
She arranged tablespoons of the dough on a pan.—1 point *(baking cookies)*

Continue play as time allows, alternating between the teams. While playing, have students discuss which clues were the most beneficial in determining the action being talked about. Also, encourage students to offer other clues that would describe the given action.

Follow-Up Discussion

Following the above activities, discuss that sometimes the activity someone is talking about is not directly stated during conversation or in a reading. However, by cuing in on the individual parts of the activity, what the person is doing can be inferred. Remind students that

BETWEEN THE LINES

they have now learned ways to infer an action. Explain that they will now have opportunities to practice this skill with the provided *Action Activity* pages.

Remember

Before using the activity pages in this section, scan the items to determine vocabulary or world knowledge that might be unfamiliar or confusing to students. Discuss these concepts before working on the inferencing activity pages. However, be careful not to inadvertently provide too much information, taking away from the individual's opportunity to figure out new word(s) or world knowledge independently.

Section 4: Action Inferences

NAME:_____ DATE:_____

Directions—Action Activity 1

For each item on this page, what someone is doing is implied. Carefully examine each item for key words or phrases that will help you infer the activity. Let's look at the example.

Example

Steve sat in the chairlift. He jumped off at the top of the mountain.
- a. What was Steve going to do? *(ski)*
- b. Which key words give you clues to Steve's activity? *(chairlift, jumped off at the top of the mountain)*

---

1 Marcel put his luggage in the overhead compartment and then took his seat.
- a. What was Marcel doing?
- b. Which key words give you clues to Marcel's activity?

2 The waves were really huge this morning. Leilani ran home to get her board.
- a. What was Leilani going to do?
- b. Which key words give you clues to Leilani's activity?

3 Martha took out her pen and checkbook. She had plenty of stamps.
- a. What was Martha going to do?
- b. Which key words give you clues to Martha's activity?

4 Jerry was walking along when a lovely melody came into his head. He went home and sat down at the piano and started to pick out some notes.
- a. What was Jerry doing?
- b. Which key words give you clues to Jerry's activity?

5 Dan read and reread the chapters in his history book. He underlined the important ideas. He studied his notes. He had to be ready for Mr. Mason's class tomorrow.
- a. What was Dan going to do tomorrow?
- b. Which key words give you clues to Dan's activity?

BETWEEN THE LINES

NAME:_____ DATE:_____

Directions—Action Activity 2

For each item on this page, what someone is doing is implied. Carefully examine each item for key words or phrases that will help you infer the activity.

1. After filling his water bottle, Jeffrey put on his helmet and gloves. He had checked his tires earlier in the day. He was looking forward to a fun-filled day.

   a. What was Jeffrey going to do?

   b. Which key words give you clues to Jeffrey's activity?

2. The jars of peanut butter and jelly were on the kitchen counter. Mom sliced four pieces of bread from the freshly baked loaf.

   a. What was Mom going to do?

   b. Which key words give you clues to Mom's activity?

3. Each person had laid their money out at the side of the board. The property cards were in the box, and a die was thrown. Janet was happy when she passed GO and collected $200 dollars.

   a. What were the people doing?

   b. Which key words give you clues to their activity?

4. Sophia preheated the oven. She stirred everything together and then added chocolate chips.

   a. What was Sophia doing?

   b. Which key words give you clues to Sophia's activity?

5. The ball came swiftly at Rita. She had her racket in position and had no trouble returning the ball within the court boundaries.

   a. What was Rita doing?

   b. Which key words give you clues to Rita's activity?

6. Tiger used the sand wedge effectively. He then reached for his putter.

   a. What was Tiger doing?

   b. Which key words give you clues to Tiger's activity?

Section 4: Action Inferences

NAME:_____ DATE:_____

Directions—Action Activity 3

For each item on this page, what someone is doing is implied. Carefully examine each item for key words or phrases that will help you infer the activity.

1 Mario took his bathing suit and headed for the YMCA.
   a. What was Mario going to do?
   b. Which key words give you clues to Mario's activity?

2 Andrew put on his coat, got the leash, and whistled.
   a. What was Andrew going to do?
   b. Which key words give you clues to Andrew's activity?

3 Jack opened the garage door and drove the car onto the driveway. He filled a bucket with soapy water and hooked up the hose.
   a. What was Jack going to do?
   b. Which key words give you clues to Jack's activity?

4 Jill cut the pattern and pinned it to the fabric. Soon she would have a teal blue linen dress just like the one she saw at the mall.
   a. What was Jill doing?
   b. Which key words give you clues to Jill's activity?

5 It was fascinating to watch Marcello tossing the dough into the air while he shaped it into a nearly perfect circle. When it was just the right size, he would put sauce and cheese on it and put it into the oven.
   a. What was Marcello doing?
   b. Which key words give you clues to Marcello's activity?

6 Jim sanded the wood until it was satiny smooth. When the piece was done, it would have five drawers, each about eight inches deep, nineteen inches long, and thirty inches wide.
   a. What was Jim doing?
   b. Which key words give you clues to Jim's activity?

BETWEEN THE LINES

NAME:_____ DATE:_____

Directions—Action Activity 4

For each item on this page, what someone is doing is implied. Carefully examine each item for key words or phrases that will help you infer the activity.

1 Katherine put on her jodhpurs and boots. The trail would be beautiful on this autumn day.

   a. What was Katherine going to do?

   b. Which key words give you clues to Katherine's activity?

2 Stefan put the beans into the grinder for about twenty seconds. He had put in just the right amount of beans to brew eight cups.

   a. What was Stefan going to doing?

   b. Which key words give you clues to Stefan's activity?

3 Carrie Ellen cut the carrots, onions, and potatoes into small chunks. She added the vegetables to the brisket in the pot, and poured in some broth.

   a. What is Carrie Ellen doing?

   b. Which key words give you clues to Carrie Ellen's activity?

4 When Shelly started, the points were dull. Now they are all ground down to little stubs. I guess she didn't know when to stop.

   a. What was Shelly doing?

   b. Which key words give you clues to Shelly's activity?

5 Lee sprayed a fine mist and then used paper towels to rub away the dirt. It certainly made a difference. Now the sunlight was streaming in.

   a. What was Lee doing?

   b. Which key words give you clues to Lee's activity?

6 Gideon cut it in half, and then cut each half into slices. It was a delicious shade of crimson red. This variety was seedless, so there was no worrying about what to do with little black seeds.

   a. What is Gideon doing?

   b. Which key words give you clues to Gideon's activity?

Section 4: Action Inferences

Answer Key

These answers are merely suggestions. The facilitator should judge if the individual's responses are appropriate for each item.

Action Activity 1 (page 49)

1. a. going on an airplane flight or a bus trip
   b. luggage, overhead compartment

2. a. go surfing
   b. waves were really huge, board

3. a. pay her bills
   b. pen, checkbook, stamps

4. a. trying to compose music or a song
   b. melody came into his head, sat down at the piano, pick out some notes

5. a. take a history test
   b. read and reread the chapters, history book, underlined the important ideas, studied his notes, class

Action Activity 2 (page 50)

1. a. go bike riding
   b. filling his water bottle; put on his helmet and gloves; tires

2. a. make sandwiches
   b. jars of peanut butter and jelly were on the kitchen counter; sliced four pieces of bread

3. a. playing Monopoly
   b. laid their money out at the side of the board; property cards; a die was thrown; passed GO and collected $200

4. a. baking cookies
   b. preheated the oven, stirred everything together, added chocolate chips

5. a. playing tennis
   b. ball came swiftly at Rita, racket, returning the ball within the court boundaries

6. a. playing golf
   b. Tiger, sand wedge, putter

BETWEEN THE LINES

Action Activity 3 (page 51)

1. a. go swimming
   b. bathing suit, YMCA

2. a. walk the dog
   b. put on his coat, got the leash, whistled

3. a. wash the car
   b. car onto the driveway, bucket with soapy water, hose

4. a. making a dress
   b. pattern, pinned it to the fabric, dress

5. a. making a pizza
   b. tossing the dough; shaped it; circle; sauce and cheese; put it into the oven

6. a. building a dresser
   b. sanded the wood, five drawers, eight inches deep, nineteen inches long, thirty inches wide

Action Activity 4 (page 52)

1. a. go horseback riding
   b. jodhpurs and boots; trail

2. a. make a pot of coffee
   b. beans, grinder, brew eight cups

3. a. making a pot roast or stew
   b. cut carrots, onions, and potatoes into small chunks; brisket; pot; broth

4. a. sharpening pencils
   b. points were dull, ground down to little stubs, didn't know when to stop

5. a. washing windows
   b. sprayed a fine mist, used paper towels to rub away the dirt, sunlight was streaming in

6. a. preparing a watermelon
   b. crimson red, variety was seedless, little black seeds

Section 5: Instrument Inferences

Warm-Ups

Before using the activity pages in this section, use the following warm-ups to teach the concept of instrument inferences.

Tool Duel

Copy and cut apart the *Tool Duel* activity cards provided in Appendix E on pages 164–167. Separate the cards into two piles: *Tools* (two of each) and *Tasks*. Organize students into teams of two and give one member of each team a stack of *Tool* cards and the other member a stack of *Task* cards. Direct students to keep their cards face-down. Have teams compete against each other as they attempt to match up tools with tasks, playing their cards as the card game War is played. When a tool and task set is turned over and matches (e.g., *scissors* and *cut hair*), the team scores a point. The team with the most points at the end of the predetermined time wins.

Tool Addition

Make a copy of the *Tool Addition* statements in Appendix E on page 168. Divide students into groups of two or three. Read one of the statements from the list. Give students one minute to write as many tools or instruments that could be used for the given task. For example: Harry painted the walls with a _____ *(roller, paintbrush, paint sprayer)*. Have teams add up the number of tools they can think of for each task presented. The team with the most points wins.

Follow-Up Discussion

Following the above activities, discuss that the tool or device a person is using is not always labeled during conversation or in a reading. However, by using the context clues regarding the work that is done with the tool, a reasonable inference can be made. Remind students that they have now learned ways to infer an instrument. Explain that they will now have opportunities to practice this skill with the provided *Instrument Activity* pages.

Remember

Before using the activity pages in this section, scan the items to determine vocabulary or world knowledge that might be unfamiliar or confusing to students. Discuss these concepts before working on the inferencing activity pages. However, be careful not to inadvertently provide too much information, taking away from the individual's opportunity to figure out new word(s) or world knowledge independently.

Between the Lines

NAME:_____ DATE:_____

Directions—Instrument Activity 1

For each item on this page, a tool or other device someone is using is implied. Carefully examine each item for key words or phrases that will help you infer the instrument being used. Let's look at the example.

Example

Jim cut the unruly hedges into a more pleasing shape.

a. What tool was Jim using? *(a hedge trimmer)*

b. Which key words give you clues to the tool Jim used? *(unruly hedges, more pleasing shape)*

---

1 Larry added more paper before he was able to finish making copies for everyone at the meeting.

a. What device was Larry using?

b. Which key words give you clues to the device Larry used?

2 The turkey was on the platter, and Dad made several slices before cutting off the leg.

a. What tool was Dad using?

b. Which key words give you clues to the tool Dad used?

3 Herb hit the ball and sent it almost 300 yards across the green.

a. What device was Herb using?

b. Which key words give you clues to the device Herb used?

4 After Barbara pressed "Save," she moved the mouse to select "Print."

a. What device was Barbara using?

b. Which key words give you clues to the device Barbara used?

5 Marina cooked the apples in a little water until they became soft. Now all she had to do was get rid of the skins and make the apples into a sauce.

a. What device will Marina use next?

b. Which key words give you clues to the device she will use?

Section 5: Instrument Inferences

NAME:_____ DATE:_____

Directions—Instrument Activity 2

For each item on this page, a tool or other device someone is using is implied. Carefully examine each item for key words or phrases that will help you infer the instrument being used.

1 When Daddy was finished, little Stephie no longer had trouble balancing her bike as she rode it.

   a. What device did Daddy put on the bike?

   b. Which key words give you clues to what device was added to Stephie's bike?

2 After she changed the flat tire, Lisa tightened the nuts on the wheel.

   a. What tool did Lisa use?

   b. Which key words give you clues to the tool Lisa used?

3 Charles's spaghetti was done, so he quickly tilted the pot and drained the water from it.

   a. What device did Charles use?

   b. Which key words give you clues to the device Charles used?

4 Styling hair can be tricky. Suzanne found that one way to get the proper shape is by using a brush and hot air.

   a. What device does Suzanne use?

   b. Which key words give you clues to the device Suzanne uses?

5 Glady finished the story and put the cursor on "Print."

   a. What device did Glady use?

   b. Which key words give you clues to the device Glady used?

6 Even on this hot summer day the soft drinks at the picnic were kept icy cold.

   a. What device was used?

   b. Which key words give you clues to the device being used?

Between the Lines © 2006 C.C. Spector. Published by Thinking Publications.
Duplication permitted for educational use only.

BETWEEN THE LINES

NAME:_____ DATE:_____

Directions—Instrument Activity 3

For each item on this page, a tool or other device someone is using is implied. Carefully examine each item for key words or phrases that will help you infer the instrument being used.

---

1. Geraldo decided to cut the grass even shorter than he did last week.

    a. What device did Geraldo use?

    b. Which key words give you clues to the device Geraldo used?

2. Jenna looked the document over carefully, and then she signed it.

    a. What device did Jenna use?

    b. Which key words give you clues to the device Jenna used?

3. Sammy passed the gravy around the table. All members of his family loved to pour lots of gravy on their roast beef.

    a. What device did Sammy pass around the table?

    b. Which key words give you clues to the device Sammy passed?

4. The men from the water company were breaking up the road to repair a damaged water pipe. The noise was deafening.

    a. What tool were the men using?

    b. Which key words give you clues to the tool the men were using?

5. For this type of chart, Robin realized that freehand drawing would not do. The lines had to be perfectly straight.

    a. What tool should Robin use to make straight lines?

    b. Which key words give you clues to the tool that Robin needed?

6. Although Lauren enjoyed eating mangoes, bits of the fruit always got stuck between her teeth. Now she would have to get them out.

    a. What tool will Lauren use to get the mango out?

    b. Which key words give you clues to the tool Lauren will use?

Section 5: Instrument Inferences

NAME:_____ DATE:_____

Directions—Instrument Activity 4

For each item on this page, a tool or other device someone is using is implied. Carefully examine each item for key words or phrases that will help you infer the instrument being used.

1 My mom gets angry because my dad loves to "channel surf."
   a. What device does Dad use?
   b. Which key words give you clues to the device Dad uses?

2 The rain hitting the windshield was no longer a drizzle. It had become quite heavy. Howard cleared the pelting water away so he would have a better view of the road.
   a. What device did Howard use?
   b. Which key words give you clues to the device Howard used?

3 After the dog and the kids ran in from the muddy yard, the kitchen floor looked very dirty. Mom managed to get it clean in just a few minutes.
   a. What device did Mom use?
   b. Which key words give you clues to the device Mom used?

4 The autumn leaves were falling so fast that they stuffed up the gutters and drainpipes. Maury had to get onto the roof to get the leaves out.
   a. What device did Maury use to get on the roof?
   b. Which key words give you clues to the device Maury used?

5 The dogs were romping in the woods. Charlie signaled the dogs that it was time for their dinner. He was glad that the dogs could hear the high-pitched sound.
   a. What device did Charlie use?
   b. Which key words give you clues to the device Charlie used?

6 Marisha rode downhill and decided to change the speed of her bike.
   a. What device was Marisha using?
   b. Which key words give you clues to the device Marisha used?

BETWEEN THE LINES

Answer Key

These answers are merely suggestions. The facilitator should judge if the individual's responses are appropriate for each item.

Instrument Activity 1 (page 56)

1. a. a copying machine
   b. added more paper, making copies

2. a. a carving knife
   b. turkey, made several slices, cutting off the leg

3. a. a golf club
   b. hit the ball, 300 yards across the green

4. a. a computer
   b. "Save," moved the mouse, "Print"

5. a. a strainer
   b. get rid of the skins, make the apples into a sauce

Instrument Activity 2 (page 57)

1. a. training wheels
   b. little, no longer had trouble balancing her bike

2. a. a wrench
   b. changed the flat tire, tightened the nuts on the wheel

3. a. a colander
   b. spaghetti, tilted the pot, drained the water

4. a. a hair blower
   b. styling hair; shape; using a brush and hot air

5. a. a mouse and/or printer
   b. put the cursor on "Print"

6. a. a cooler or ice chest
   b. soft drinks, picnic, kept icy cold

Section 5: Instrument Inferences

Instrument Activity 3 (page 58)

1. a. a lawn mower
   b. cut the grass, shorter

2. a. a pen
   b. document, signed it

3. a. a gravy boat or a ladle
   b. pour, gravy

4. a. a jackhammer
   b. breaking up the road, noise was deafening

5. a. a ruler
   b. lines, perfectly straight

6. a. dental floss or a toothpick
   b. bits of fruit, stuck between her teeth, get them out

Instrument Activity 4 (page 59)

1. a. a remote control
   b. "channel surf"

2. a. the windshield wipers
   b. rain hitting the windshield, cleared the pelting water away

3. a. a mop
   b. muddy, floor looked very dirty, get it clean

4. a. a ladder
   b. gutters and drainpipes; get onto the roof

5. a. dog whistle
   b. signaled the dogs, dogs could hear the high-pitched sound

6. a. the gearshift
   b. change the speed of her bike

Section 6: Category Inferences

Warm-Ups

Before using the activity pages in this section, use the following warm-ups to teach the concept of category inferences.

Category Stack-Up Race

Copy and cut apart the *Category Stack-Up Race* cards provided in Appendix F on pages 169–173. They contain *Category Name* cards (e.g., *Bodies of Water*) and *Category Member* cards (e.g., *ocean, creek*). The *Category Name* cards are larger than the *Category Member* cards. Place the *Category Name* cards around the room on tables, desks, and counters. Distribute the *Category Member* cards, giving each student the same number. Tell the students when to start, and direct them to race to place their member cards on the appropriate category piles. Following the game, talk about each category and its members. Discuss how decisions were made regarding which cards belonged to each category. If any cards were placed incorrectly, discuss the correct category and what makes the member belong.

VARIATION: If the group is too large to all race at once, divide the group into teams. Conduct the competition like a relay; the first person in the line puts the top card on the appropriate category and then hands the stack to the next person.

Class Classification

Copy and cut apart the *Class Classification* cards provided in Appendix F on pages 174–175. Divide the group into two teams. Select a card and call out the category. Direct teams to work together to write as many items that belong to the category as possible within a one-minute time period. When time is up, have teams read their lists. As a group, judge the appropriateness of the items listed. Award teams one point for each acceptable item. Continue the game as long as time permits. The team with the most points at the end of the game wins.

Follow-Up Discussion

Following the above activities, discuss that sometimes during a conversation or in a reading items will be talked about that belong in a group. In this situation it is important to infer what category is being talked about in order to make appropriate contributions to the conversation. Suggest that when adding to a conversation, it is important to speak about information that belongs to the same category. Remind students that they have now learned ways to infer a category. Explain that they will now have opportunities to practice this skill with the provided *Category Activity* pages.

BETWEEN THE LINES

Remember

Before using the activity pages in this section, scan the items to determine vocabulary or world knowledge that might be unfamiliar or confusing to students. Discuss these concepts before working on the inferencing activity pages. However, be careful not to inadvertently provide too much information, taking away from the individual's opportunity to figure out new word(s) or world knowledge independently.

Section 6: Category Inferences

NAME:_____ DATE:_____

Directions—Category Activity 1

For each sentence on this page, several words that belong to a particular category are underlined. Carefully examine the underlined words and decide a category for each group. Let's look at the example.

Example

The broccoli, spinach, and sweet peas were brought in fresh every day.

Category: *(green vegetables)*

---

1 I have a friend who can't decide which is her favorite—blonde, brunette, or auburn.

Category:

2 The mare, stallion, and colt were running together.

Category:

3 Joan becomes frightened at the very thought of tornadoes, hurricanes, or floods.

Category:

4 With her perm, Jill looked like a few of the other girls. The two guys, on the other hand, looked very different. One had a ponytail, the other a crew cut.

Category:

5 In her closet, Beth had minis, ankle lengths, and knee lengths.

Category:

6 My sister likes whole or 2%, but I prefer skim.

Category:

7 In class yesterday, we learned about the Nile, the Swanee, and the Mississippi.

Category:

8 My dad often has to wear button-down or dress, but he prefers short-sleeved.

Category:

BETWEEN THE LINES

NAME:_____ DATE:_____

Directions—Category Activity 2

For each sentence on this page, several words that belong to a particular category are underlined. Carefully examine the underlined words and decide a category for each group.

1 I really love <u>raisins</u>, <u>prunes</u>, and <u>currants</u>.
   Category:

2 Three of the best are <u>Cruise</u>, <u>Depp</u>, and <u>Pitt</u>.
   Category:

3 After I moved, I had to find a new <u>doctor</u>, <u>lawyer</u>, and <u>accountant</u>.
   Category:

4 They had fresh <u>grapes</u>, <u>plums</u>, and <u>apricots</u> yesterday.
   Category:

5 My sister, brother, and I are all different. She's a <u>Gemini</u>, he's a <u>Taurus</u>, and I'm a <u>Leo</u>.
   Category:

6 I especially enjoyed seeing <u>*The Alien*</u>, <u>*ET*</u>, and <u>*Star Wars*</u>.
   Category:

7 I love <u>salty pretzels</u> or <u>potato chips</u>, but my friend would rather have <u>buttered popcorn</u>.
   Category:

8 <u>Great Danes</u> and <u>golden retrievers</u> are rather large to have in small apartments. It would probably be wiser to have a <u>miniature poodle</u>.
   Category:

Section 6: Category Inferences

NAME:_____ DATE:_____

Directions—Category Activity 3

For each sentence on this page, several words that belong to a particular category are underlined. Carefully examine the underlined words and decide a category for each group.

1 Any time you go to the Galapagos Islands you are likely to see many <u>terns</u> and <u>herons</u>, but you have to go at specific times of the year to see an <u>albatross</u>.
   Category:

2 I don't mind <u>sole</u> or <u>flounder</u>, but <u>trout</u> has too many bones.
   Category:

3 <u>Oak</u> is one of the hardest, but many manufacturers frequently prefer to use <u>cedar</u> or <u>pine</u>.
   Category:

4 I'm rather old-fashioned. I still like the <u>fox trot</u> and the <u>rumba</u>. Even though I'm crazy about the <u>tango</u>, I think it takes experts to do it well.
   Category:

5 The sounds made by a <u>violin</u>, a <u>cello</u>, and a <u>bass fiddle</u> can be truly beautiful.
   Category:

6 When I was a child, I had the <u>measles</u>, <u>chicken pox</u>, and the <u>mumps</u>.
   Category:

7 <u>Hagar the Horrible</u>, <u>Dennis the Menace</u>, and <u>Peanuts</u> are three of the best.
   Category:

8 My mother has an <u>emerald</u> and a <u>sapphire</u>. She would love to add a <u>ruby</u> to her collection.
   Category:

BETWEEN THE LINES

NAME:_____ DATE:_____

Directions—Category Activity 4

For each sentence on this page, several words that belong to a particular category are underlined. Carefully examine the underlined words and decide a category for each group.

1. Birthdays are usually a cause for underlined{happiness} and underlined{joy}, but some people actually underlined{abhor} them.
Category:

2. When given a choice, my parents prefer to go to the underlined{Atlantic} rather than the underlined{Pacific}. I personally prefer the underlined{Indian}.
Category:

3. The clean underlined{sheets} and underlined{pillowcases} were put on first, then the underlined{blankets}.
Category:

4. After flipping through the underlined{magazine} at the dentist's office, I picked up a underlined{newspaper} to see if they had a underlined{book} review section.
Category:

5. Before the underlined{zipper} was invented in 1913, people used underlined{buttons}. Nowadays many manufacturers use underlined{Velcro}.
Category:

6. I couldn't find underlined{clippers} or a underlined{file}, so I used an underlined{emery} board.
Category:

7. I used a little underlined{magenta} and underlined{puce}, and a lot of underlined{ocher}.
Category:

8. I love underlined{pistachio}, but I'd settle for underlined{chocolate} or underlined{strawberry}.
Category:

Section 6: Category Inferences

Answer Key

These answers are merely suggestions. The facilitator should judge if the individual's responses are appropriate for each item.

Category Activity 1 (page 65)

1. hair colors
2. horses
3. natural disasters
4. hairstyles
5. skirts or dresses
6. kinds of milk
7. rivers
8. shirts

Category Activity 2 (page 66)

1. dried fruits
2. actors
3. professionals
4. fruits
5. astrological signs
6. science fiction films
7. snack foods
8. dogs

Category Activity 3 (page 67)

1. sea birds
2. fish
3. woods used to make furniture
4. dances
5. stringed instruments
6. diseases (illnesses)
7. comic strips
8. precious gems

BETWEEN THE LINES

Category Activity 4 (page 68)

1. emotions, feelings
2. oceans
3. bedding
4. reading material
5. fasteners for clothing
6. things to shorten or shape one's nails
7. colors
8. ice cream flavors

Section 7: Object Inferences

Warm-Ups

Before using the activity pages in this section, use the following warm-ups to teach the concept of object inferences.

Twenty Questions

Copy and cut apart the *Twenty Questions* cards in Appendix G on pages 176–177. To illustrate the possible aspects of an object, play the game Twenty Questions. Divide students into pairs. Give each pair a pile of *Twenty Questions* cards. Direct one student from each pair to choose a card and tell to what category the object belongs. The other student should ask *yes/no* questions that will help him or her to guess the object. For example, if the student picked the word *cow*:

Category: Animal

Is it bigger than me?	Yes
Does it live in the jungle?	No
Does it live on a farm?	Yes
Does it give milk?	Yes
Is it a cow?	Yes!

Hot Potato

Gather a supply of small, nonbreakable objects (e.g., ball, stuffed animals, eraser). Have students sit in a circle. Give one of the objects to a student. Direct the student to toss the item to another student. The student that catches the item must describe the item in some way (i.e., category, physical attribute, function). Continue tossing this item for several turns, then replace it with another item. Continue as time allows.

Follow-Up Discussion

Following the above activities, discuss that sometimes the name of an object is not given during a conversation or in a reading. However, by using its descriptors one can figure out (infer) what is being talked about. Remind students that they have now learned ways to infer an object. Explain that they will now have opportunities to practice this skill with the provided *Object Activity* pages.

Remember

Before using the activity pages in this section, scan the items to determine vocabulary or world knowledge that might be unfamiliar or confusing to students. Discuss these concepts before working on the inferencing activity pages. However, be careful not to inadvertently provide too much information, taking away from the individual's opportunity to figure out new word(s) or world knowledge independently.

BETWEEN THE LINES

NAME:_____ DATE:_____

Directions—Object Activity 1

For each item on this page, an object being talked about is implied. Carefully examine each item for key words or phrases that will help you infer the object. Let's look at the example.

Example

When June dropped it, it broke into a hundred pieces, and the milk spilled all over the floor.

    a. What did June drop? *(a glass or bottle)*

    b. Which key words give you clues to what object was dropped? *(dropped it, broke, milk spilled)*

---

1 John corrected his mistakes and then brushed away the bits of rubber on the paper.
    a. What is being talked about?
    b. Which key words give you clues to the item being talked about?

2 Margaret put the tomatoes, tomato puree, onions, garlic, and spices in a pot and let them simmer slowly for an hour.
    a. What is being talked about?
    b. Which key words give you clues to the item being talked about?

3 When Grace was through using it in the shower, her hair was soft, shiny, and smelled great.
    a. What is being talked about?
    b. Which key words give you clues to the item being talked about?

4 Rebecca slathered it on generously before she went out into the sun.
    a. What is being talked about?
    b. Which key words give you clues to the item being talked about?

5 Eric took out a new reed and put it in the mouthpiece. Then he polished the ebony wood.
    a. What is being talked about?
    b. Which key words give you clues to the item being talked about?

Section 7: Object Inferences

NAME:_____ DATE:_____

Directions—Object Activity 2

For each item on this page, an object being talked about is implied. Carefully examine each item for key words or phrases that will help you infer the object.

1 Mona said I looked like a cow chewing her cud, so I got rid of it in a trashcan.
   a. What is being talked about?
   b. Which key words give you clues to the item being talked about?

2 After checking the wind, Karen decided to put up the spinnaker. She set a course for Tahiti.
   a. What is being talked about?
   b. Which key words give you clues to the item being talked about?

3 So many people talk on them wherever you go. They use them in supermarkets, in their cars, at the bank, and even in restrooms. It makes you wonder what people did before they were invented.
   a. What is being talked about?
   b. Which key words give you clues to the item being talked about?

4 Rich put 10 gallons of gas in its tank and checked the oil before going to the office.
   a. What is being talked about?
   b. Which key words give you clues to the item being talked about?

5 Mark took off the lid and put in another seashell for his collection.
   a. What is being talked about?
   b. Which key words give you clues to the item being talked about?

6 William practiced every day for weeks, especially the black keys, until finally he could play the music with both hands.
   a. What is being talked about?
   b. Which key words give you clues to the item being talked about?

BETWEEN THE LINES

NAME:_____ DATE:_____

Directions—Object Activity 3

For each item on this page, an object being talked about is implied. Carefully examine each item for key words or phrases that will help you infer the object.

1 Veronica took one and asked Donna to use the other one. Between the two of them, they managed to row the boat.
   a. What is being talked about?
   b. Which key words give you clues to the items being talked about?

2 It's a good thing Maria had one in the trunk of the car. Now she would be able to lift up the car and put on the spare tire.
   a. What is being talked about?
   b. Which key words give you clues to the item being talked about?

3 After Zoë used it to spread the icing on the cake, she washed it and put it back in the drawer.
   a. What is being talked about?
   b. Which key words give you clues to the item being talked about?

4 It's a good thing Ariel had some more in the tent. It would be awful to be out in the woods at night with a flashlight that didn't work.
   a. What is being talked about?
   b. Which key words give you clues to the item being talked about?

5 The water was coming out of the hose too fast, so Gil gave it a few turns to slow down the stream.
   a. What is being talked about?
   b. Which key words give you clues to the item being talked about?

6 The whistling let Julie know that the water was boiling. Now she could make some tea.
   a. What is being talked about?
   b. Which key words give you clues to the item being talked about?

Section 7: Object Inferences

NAME:_____ DATE:_____

Directions—Object Activity 4

For each item on this page, an object being talked about is implied. Carefully examine each item for key words or phrases that will help you infer the object.

1 Two of Dracula's were long, pointy, and very sharp.
   a. What is being talked about?
   b. Which key words give you clues to the items being talked about?

2 Damien, the barber, made sure they were always sharp. When they were dull he could not give his customers a close shave.
   a. What is being talked about?
   b. Which key words give you clues to the items being talked about?

3 Erica used them to hold her hair back because she couldn't find her barrettes.
   a. What is being talked about?
   b. Which key words give you clues to the items being talked about?

4 Just because the three little kittens lost them, the mama cat didn't let them have any pie.
   a. What is being talked about?
   b. Which key words give you clues to the items being talked about?

5 Dad was always losing them, even though there was a hook for them by the garage door. Now how would we drive to Grandma's house?
   a. What is being talked about?
   b. Which key words give you clues to the items being talked about?

6 After Marcie wrote down her secret thoughts for the day, she locked it and hid it at the bottom of her drawer.
   a. What is being talked about?
   b. Which key words give you clues to the item being talked about?

BETWEEN THE LINES

Answer Key

These answers are merely suggestions. The facilitator should judge whether the individual's responses are appropriate for each item.

Object Activity 1 (page 72)

1. a. an eraser
   b. corrected his mistakes, bits of rubber on the paper

2. a. tomato sauce or spaghetti sauce
   b. tomatoes, tomato puree, onions, garlic, and spices; pot; simmer slowly

3. a. shampoo or conditioner
   b. hair; soft, shiny, and smelled great

4. a. sunscreen
   b. slathered it on, before, into the sun

5. a. a clarinet
   b. reed, mouthpiece, ebony wood

Object Activity 2 (page 73)

1. a. gum
   b. chewing, got rid of it in a trashcan

2. a. a sailboat
   b. checking the wind, spinnaker, set a course

3. a. cell phones
   b. talk on them; use them in supermarkets, in their cars, at the bank and even in restrooms

4. a. an automobile
   b. gas in its tank, checked the oil

5. a. a container
   b. took off the lid, put in

6. a. a keyboard
   b. practiced, the black keys, play the music with both hands

Section 7: Object Inferences

Object Activity 3 (page 74)

1. a. oars or paddles
   b. took one, use the other, row the boat

2. a. a jack
   b. trunk of the car, lift up the car, put on the spare tire

3. a. a spatula or knife
   b. spread the icing on the cake, back in the drawer

4. a. batteries or flashlights
   b. out in the woods at night, a flashlight that didn't work

5. a. a nozzle
   b. water was coming out of the hose, gave it a few turns to slow down the stream

6. a. a teakettle
   b. whistling, water was boiling, make some tea

Object Activity 4 (page 75)

1. a. fangs or teeth
   b. Dracula; long, pointy, and very sharp

2. a. razor blades
   b. barber, sharp, dull, customers a close shave

3. a. combs or rubber bands
   b. hold her hair back, couldn't find her barrettes

4. a. mittens
   b. three little kittens lost them, mama cat didn't let them have any pie

5. a. car keys
   b. always losing them, a hook for them by the garage door, drive

6. a. a diary
   b. wrote down her secret thoughts, locked it, hid it

Section 8: Feelings Inferences

Warm-Ups

Before using the activity pages in this section, use the following activities to teach the concept of feelings inferences.

Brainstorming

Use brainstorming to raise awareness of the vast amount of feelings words we have in our language. Often, students we work with are limited in their expressive vocabulary in this area, using only words such as *happy, sad,* and *mad*. Ask students to think of words for different kinds of feelings. Make a list of these words; encourage the use of a thesaurus to help generate a longer list. Discuss what might cause a person to have a particular feeling on the list. For example, happiness might be caused by getting 100 percent on a difficult math exam. Sadness might be caused by the loss of a beloved pet.

Expressions

Copy and cut apart the *Expressions* cards in Appendix H on page 178. On each card a different feeling or emotion is written. Have students take turns selecting one of the cards. Instruct students to act out emotions using facial expressions, gestures, and body language. Have other students guess which emotion is being displayed. (This activity is particularly helpful for individuals with disorders in the autism spectrum such as Asperger's syndrome.)

Follow-Up Discussion

After completing these activities, discuss that we do not always know what people are feeling. However, by evaluating their situations, facial expressions, gestures, and body language we can infer how they are feeling. Explain that inferences of feelings often rely on personal experiences. If a given situation makes a person feel anger, it can be inferred that the same situation would make another individual feel anger as well. Also, discuss the fact that although many feelings are common to most people, some are unique to an individual. For example, being elected president of a prestigious club would cause most people to say they feel elation, happiness, or pride. If the terms used are *worried, scared,* or *overwhelmed,* explore reasons why these terms were selected. The individual might feel that holding the office of president of the club is too daunting a task or too time consuming. Mention that inferring another person's feelings is not always an easy task. However, remind students that they have now learned ways to infer a feeling. Explain that they will now have opportunities to practice this skill with the provided *Feelings Activity* pages.

BETWEEN THE LINES

Remember

Before using the activity pages in this section, scan the items to determine vocabulary or world knowledge that might be unfamiliar or confusing to students. Discuss these concepts before working on the inferencing activity pages. However, be careful not to inadvertently provide too much information, taking away from the individual's opportunity to figure out new word(s) or world knowledge independently.

Section 8: Feelings Inferences

NAME:_____ DATE:_____

Directions—Feelings Activity 1

For each item on this page, someone's feelings are implied. Carefully examine each item for key words or phrases that will help you infer the feeling. Let's look at the example.

Example

Joanne saw Marion wearing a new green dress. It was the same dress she had pointed out to Marion at the mall. She had told Marion she was saving up to buy it.

   a. What feeling(s) might Joanne have experienced? *(anger, betrayal)*
   b. Which key words give you clues to why she might feel this way? *(same dress she had pointed out to Marion at the mall, she was saving up to buy it)*
   c. Explain a time when something like this happened to you. How did you feel?

---

1 Marcia winced as she slipped and landed on the ice. Steve quickly rushed over to help her get up. She blushed as she took his hand.

   a. What feeling(s) might Marcia have experienced?
   b. Which words give you a clue for why she may have felt this way?
   c. Explain a time when you felt this way.

2 For the fourth time in five minutes, Sparky asked Charlie if he could borrow his eraser.

   a. What feeling(s) might Charlie have experienced?
   b. Which words give you a clue for why he may have felt this way?
   c. Explain a time when you felt this way.

3 Jeannie and Chloe were best friends. They both had a crush on Lonnie. Lonnie asked Chloe to go to the prom.

   a. What feeling(s) might Jeannie have experienced?
   b. Which words give you a clue for why she may have felt this way?
   c. Have you ever felt this way about one of your friends? Explain why.

4 All the kids laughed at Ted whenever he made a mistake in school. They teased him on the playground and purposely pushed him during gym class.

   a. What feeling(s) might Ted have experienced?
   b. Which words give you a clue for why he may have felt this way?
   c. Have you ever been laughed at or teased? How did it make you feel?

Between the Lines © 2006 C.C. Spector. Published by Thinking Publications.
Duplication permitted for educational use only.

BETWEEN THE LINES

NAME:_____ DATE:_____

Directions—Feelings Activity 2

For each item on this page, someone's feelings are implied. Carefully examine each item for key words or phrases that will help you infer the feeling.

1 Anthony lost his job after working at the company for 24 years. In one more year he could have retired with a nice pension.
   a. What feeling(s) might Anthony have experienced?
   b. Which words give you a clue for why he may have felt this way?
   c. Has anyone ever taken away one of your responsibilities? How did you feel?

2 It was the night before Thanksgiving and Tina had worked all day on dinner preparations for the 18 guests who would be there the next day.
   a. What feeling(s) might Tina have experienced?
   b. Which words give you a clue for why she may have felt this way?
   c. Have you ever planned a large party? How did it make you feel?

3 After a delicious dinner, Jon watched his favorite TV program.
   a. What feeling(s) might Jon have experienced?
   b. Which words give you a clue for why he may have felt this way?
   c. What activity makes you feel this way?

4 Martin had practiced his Mozart piece for many hours before the piano recital, but he still made three mistakes.
   a. What feeling(s) might Martin have experienced?
   b. Which words give you a clue for why he may have felt this way?
   c. Explain a time when you worked hard at something, and it still didn't go as planned. How did you feel?

5 Every year Juliana ran the 100 meter race and every year she came in second. This year she won!
   a. What feeling(s) might Juliana have experienced?
   b. Which words give you a clue for why she may have felt this way?
   c. Have you ever won a competition? How did you feel?

Section 8: Feelings Inferences

NAME:_____ DATE:_____

Directions—Feelings Activity 3

For each item on this page, someone's feelings are implied. Carefully examine each item for key words or phrases that will help you infer the feeling.

1 The cold, snowy days of winter seemed endless. Meredith thought about her last vacation in the Caribbean.
   a. What feeling(s) might Meredith have experienced?
   b. Which words give you a clue for why she may have felt this way?
   c. Have you ever wished you could be somewhere else? Explain why.

2 There was so much left to do. Karl estimated it would take at least three more days to finish all of his work, but he only had one.
   a. What feeling(s) might Karl have experienced?
   b. Which words give you a clue for why he may have felt this way?
   c. Have you ever been given a task that you didn't think you could get done? How did it make you feel?

3 Dane, as usual, took the largest slice of pie.
   a. What feeling(s) might Dane have experienced?
   b. Which words give you a clue for why he may have felt this way?
   c. Have you ever felt this way? Explain when.

4 Delicious aromas wafted in from the kitchen. It would be hours before Janelle's dinner would be ready.
   a. What feeling(s) might Janelle have experienced?
   b. Which words give you a clue for why she may have felt this way?
   c. Explain a time when you just couldn't wait for something.

5 Kenneth was sure he left his wallet on the kitchen counter. When he returned to the kitchen the wallet wasn't there. Joe said he didn't see the wallet.
   a. What feeling(s) might Kenneth have experienced?
   b. Which words give you a clue for why he may have felt this way?
   c. Have you ever lost something important to you? How did it make you feel?

BETWEEN THE LINES

NAME:_____ DATE:_____

Directions—Feelings Activity 4

For each item on this page, someone's feelings are implied. Carefully examine each item for key words or phrases that will help you infer the feeling.

1 At their 25th wedding anniversary dinner, Karen and Bill talked about the early years of their marriage. They reminisced about past ski trips, picnics in the park, and the many candlelit evenings spent at home.

   a. What feeling(s) might Karen and Bill have experienced?
   b. Which words give you a clue for why they may have felt this way?
   c. How do you feel when you talk to your friends about something you did together in the past?

2 Lana kept glancing behind her as she jogged down the dark, deserted road.

   a. What feeling(s) might Lana have experienced?
   b. Which words give you a clue for why she may have felt this way?
   c. Have you ever felt this way?

3 Charlotte was deep in thought while driving downtown. Unfortunately, she didn't stop in time to avoid hitting another car's bumper.

   a. What feeling(s) might Charlotte have experienced?
   b. Which words give you a clue for why she may have felt this way?
   c. How would you feel if this happened to you?

4 After dating Daphne for almost two years, Peter decided to take her to their favorite restaurant to "pop the question."

   a. What feeling(s) might Peter have experienced?
   b. Which words give you a clue for why he may have felt this way?
   c. Explain a time when you were very nervous.

5 When Josephina finished the book, she decided to recommend it to all of her friends.

   a. What feeling(s) might Josephina have experienced?
   b. Which words give you a clue for why she may have felt this way?
   c. Tell about a product you felt this way about.

Section 8: Feelings Inferences

NAME:_____ DATE:_____

| Directions—Feelings Activity 5 |

For each item on this page, someone's feelings are implied. Carefully examine each item for key words or phrases that will help you infer the feeling.

1 Rachel just won the lottery!
   a. What feeling(s) might Rachel have experienced?
   b. Which words give you a clue for why she may have felt this way?
   c. Have you ever won something? How did it make you feel?

2 Everything seemed to be going wrong for Mary. First her car was stolen, and then her son ran away from home.
   a. What feeling(s) might Mary have experienced?
   b. Which words give you a clue for why she may have felt this way?
   c. Explain a time when you felt this way.

3 Carolyn was finally going on her long-awaited trip to Hawaii.
   a. What feeling(s) might Carolyn have experienced?
   b. Which words give you a clue for why she may have felt this way?
   c. How do you feel before going on a vacation?

4 The line at the supermarket was so long that Sylvia didn't know if she would be home in time to meet her children's school bus.
   a. What feeling(s) might Sylvia have experienced?
   b. Which words give you a clue for why she may have felt this way?
   c. How do you feel if you're running late for something?

5 Hugo couldn't stop looking at the letter. He read it over and over again. He had gotten into Blakely College, his top choice.
   a. What feeling(s) might he have experienced?
   b. Which words give you a clue for why he may have felt this way.
   c. How would you feel if this happened to you?

Between the Lines © 2006 C.C. Spector. Published by Thinking Publications.
Duplication permitted for educational use only.

85

BETWEEN THE LINES

Answer Key

These answers are merely suggestions. The facilitator should judge if the individual's responses are appropriate for each item. Note that since letter c responses are individual to each student, no suggestions are given.

Feelings Activity 1 (page 81)

1. a. pain, embarrassment
   b. winced; slipped and landed on the ice; blushed

2. a. annoyance
   b. fourth time in five minutes

3. a. jealousy, sadness
   b. they both had a crush on Lonnie, Lonnie asked Chloe to go to the prom

4. a. helplessness, humiliation, insecurity
   b. kids laughed, whenever he made a mistake, teased him, purposely pushed him

Feelings Activity 2 (page 82)

1. a. anger, fear, frustration
   b. lost his job, could have retired with a nice pension

2. a. fatigue, anticipation
   b. worked all day on dinner preparations for 18 guests

3. a. contentment
   b. delicious dinner, watched his favorite TV program

4. a. disappointment, embarrassment, frustration
   b. practiced, many hours, still made three mistakes

5. a. happiness, pride
   b. every year she came in second, she won

Feelings Activity 3 (page 83)

1. a. longing, sadness, disgust
   b. cold, snowy days of winter seemed endless; thought about her last vacation in the Caribbean

2. a. worry, pressure, nervousness, fear
   b. so much left to do, would take at least three more days, only had one

Section 8: Feelings Inferences

3. a. greed, hunger
   b. as usual; took the largest slice of pie

4. a. hunger, anticipation, annoyance
   b. it would be hours before Janelle's dinner would be ready

5. a. suspicion, worry, concern
   b. sure he left his wallet on the kitchen counter, when he returned to the kitchen the wallet wasn't there, Joe said he didn't see the wallet

Feelings Activity 4 (page 84)

1. a. nostalgia, wistfulness, contentment
   b. 25th wedding anniversary, early years, reminisced

2. a. fear, apprehension, worry
   b. kept glancing behind her; jogged down the dark, deserted road

3. a. surprise, dismay, concern
   b. deep in thought while driving, didn't stop in time, hitting another car's bumper

4. a. nervousness, hope, excitement, fear
   b. "pop the question"

5. a. appreciation, enjoyment, satisfaction
   b. finished the book, decided to recommend it to all of her friends

Feelings Activity 5 (page 85)

1. a. elation, joy
   b. won the lottery

2. a. sadness, depression, worry
   b. going wrong, her car was stolen, her son ran away from home

3. a. excitement, anticipation, happiness
   b. finally going on her long-awaited trip, Hawaii

4. a. nervousness, impatience, concern
   b. line at the supermarket was so long, didn't know if she would be home in time to meet her children's school bus

5. a. disbelief, amazement, joy
   b. he had gotten into Blakely College, his top choice

Section 9: Cause and Effect Inferences

Warm-Ups

Before using the activity pages in this section, use the following warm-ups to teach the concept of cause and effect inferences.

Why?

Copy the *Why?* statements provided in Appendix I on page 179. Arrange students in two teams. Before beginning this activity, explain to students that many different situations could cause the same outcome. For this activity, students are to think of a variety of reasons why something may have happened. Read the various statements, giving students a minute or two to write as many responses as possible for each. Teams receive one point for each appropriate answer. Continue reading situations and allowing students to write responses as time allows. The team with the most points at the end wins. Here is an example:

Her face turned bright red. Why?

1. *She slipped and everyone saw her underwear.*
2. *She was running and she got hot.*
3. *She was sick and her fever made her warm.*

And On and On and On…

Copy the *And On and On and On…* statements provided in Appendix I on page 180. Before completing this activity explain to students that every event can cause multiple consequences. To highlight this endless process write a cause where everyone can see (like on an overhead projector or dry-erase board). Discuss the multitude of consequences that may result from one event, and write these chains of responses for all to see. For example:

What would happen if you fell into a puddle?

1. *You would get wet.*
2. *Your clothes could get ruined.*
3. *You may need to go home to change clothes.*
4. *You may need to do a load of laundry.*

Continue in the same fashion with the statements provided. Continually discuss with students how one event can have consequences that go on and on and on.

Follow-Up Discussion

Following the above activities, discuss that often in a conversation or in a reading only one part of what happened is stated. It is not always clear why something happened or its

BETWEEN THE LINES

outcomes. In this situation, it is important to search our background knowledge to infer why something happened or its possible effects. Remind students that they have now learned ways to infer a cause or effect. Explain that they will now have opportunities to practice this skill with the provided *Cause and Effect Activity* pages.

Remember

Before using the activity pages in this section, scan the items to determine vocabulary or world knowledge that might be unfamiliar or confusing to students. Discuss these concepts before working on the inferencing activity pages. However, be careful not to inadvertently provide too much information, taking away from the individual's opportunity to figure out new word(s) or world knowledge independently.

Section 9: Cause and Effect Inferences

NAME:_____ DATE:_____

Directions—Cause and Effect Activity 1

For each item on this page, the reason something happened or how something will turn out is implied. Carefully examine each item for key words or phrases that will help you infer the cause and effect. Let's look at the example.

Example

All evening Mark heard the distant rumbling of thunder. The next morning he was dismayed to see a burnt tree lying across his driveway.

   a. What caused this situation? *(Lightning struck the trees.)*
   b. Which key words give you clues to the cause? *(rumbling of thunder, burnt tree lying across his driveway)*
   c. How might the fallen tree affect Mark? *(He can't get out of his driveway because it is blocked by the tree. He'll be late for work.)*

---

1 The houses near the river all had several feet of water in their basements.
   a. What caused this situation?
   b. Which key words give you clues to the cause?
   c. What will happen to the basements with water in them?

2 Molly had cookies baking in the oven. Suddenly the smoke detector went off.
   a. What caused this to happen?
   b. Which key words give you clues to the cause?
   c. How will the smoke affect Molly's house?

3 Skipper left muddy paw prints on the shiny kitchen floor.
   a. What caused this to happen?
   b. Which key words give you clues to the cause?
   c. How might Skipper's mess affect his owner's plans for the day?

4 Camille looked in the mirror and then called the hairdresser for an appointment.
   a. What caused this to happen?
   b. Which key words give you clues to the cause?
   c. How will Camille's new hairstyle affect how she feels?

Between the Lines © 2006 C.C. Spector. Published by Thinking Publications.
Duplication permitted for educational use only.

BETWEEN THE LINES

NAME:_____ DATE:_____

Directions—Cause and Effect Activity 2

For each item on this page, the reason something happened or how something will turn out is implied. Carefully examine each item for key words or phrases that will help you infer the cause and effect.

1 Tim had mowed lawns all day. The last lawn didn't look nearly as good as the first.
   a. What caused this to happen?
   b. Which key words give you clues to the cause?
   c. How might this affect Tim's future job offers?

2 Sally raked leaves into piles for more than an hour before lunch. When her dad got home from work, he scolded her for not raking the leaves.
   a. What caused this to happen?
   b. Which key words give you clues to the cause?
   c. How might this affect how Sally takes care of leaves in the future?

3 June and Benjamin spent several winter evenings deciding where to go for their summer vacation. Finally, they saw a travel agent, made all the arrangements, and paid for the trip. Sadly, they ended up staying home all summer.
   a. What caused this to happen?
   b. Which key words give you clues to the cause?
   c. How might this affect how they plan vacations in the future?

4 Amanda needed to look up a word in the dictionary. She couldn't seem to find the word.
   a. What caused this to happen?
   b. Which key words give you clues to the cause?
   c. How might this affect Amanda's dictionary use in the future?

5 The winter was especially cold, with lots of snow. Cal decided to go skiing. He came back from his skiing trip with a cast on his left leg.
   a. What caused this to happen?
   b. Which key words give you clues to the cause?
   c. How might this affect Cal at home, work, or school?

Section 9: Cause and Effect Inferences

NAME:_____ DATE:_____

Directions—Cause and Effect Activity 3

For each item on this page, the reason something happened or how something will turn out is implied. Carefully examine each item for key words or phrases that will help you infer the cause and effect.

1. Irene couldn't remember whether she took her medication when she woke up in the morning. She decided to take it before lunch. Irene ended up in the hospital.
   a. What caused this to happen?
   b. Which key words give you clues to the cause?
   c. How might this affect Irene's health?

2. Terri and Bruce spent three glorious weeks on a cruise. When they returned home, they were dismayed to see that all of their houseplants were withered and dying.
   a. What caused this to happen?
   b. Which key words give you clues to the cause?
   c. How will this affect the plants' lives?

3. Milton was in the waiting room of his dentist's office. He started reading an article in a magazine, but he was not able to finish the article.
   a. What caused this to happen?
   b. Which key words give you clues to the cause?
   c. How might this affect Milton's day?

4. Renee felt her cat, Mickey, rubbing up against her legs as she dried the crystal glasses. The phone rang and Renee ran to answer it. Suddenly Renee heard the sound of breaking glass.
   a. What caused this to happen?
   b. Which key words give you clues to the cause?
   c. How might this affect Renee?

5. The ice cream truck drove by, playing its usual melodic tune, and woke Jordan from his nap. Jordan ran to his mother.
   a. What caused this to happen?
   b. Which key words give you clues to the cause?
   c. How might this shortened nap affect Jordan?

Between the Lines © 2006 C.C. Spector. Published by Thinking Publications.
Duplication permitted for educational use only.

93

BETWEEN THE LINES

NAME:_____ DATE:_____

Directions—Cause and Effect Activity 4

For each item on this page, the reason something happened or how something will turn out is implied. Carefully examine each item for key words or phrases that will help you infer the cause and effect.

1. Goose drank some orange juice for energy. Today was the big game. He took a practice swing with his bat before walking out the kitchen door. Juice ended up all over the kitchen floor.
   a. What caused this to happen?
   b. Which key words give you clues to the cause?
   c. How might this affect Goose's morning?

2. Lolita was late for work. She had to ask her next-door neighbor to come and watch her baby, Lulu.
   a. What caused this to happen?
   b. Which key words give you clues to the cause?
   c. How might this affect Lolita at work?

3. Josh studied for days for the biology exam. He was the first one to leave the room where the test was given.
   a. What caused this to happen?
   b. Which key words give you clues to the cause?
   c. What is the likely affect of Josh's studying?

4. Yolanda was glad she remembered to bring her camera to her son's graduation ceremony. She asked all of her son's friends to pose with him for pictures. She ended up with no pictures of graduation day.
   a. What caused this to happen?
   b. Which key words give you clues to the cause?
   c. How might this affect Yolanda's memory of her son's graduation?

5. Igor had just arrived from Moscow. This was his first trip to the United States. At the airport he approached several people to ask for directions to the baggage claim area. No one was able to help him.
   a. What caused this to happen?
   b. Which key words give you clues to the cause?
   c. How might this affect Igor's impression of the United States?

Section 9: Cause and Effect Inferences

NAME:_____ DATE:_____

Directions—Cause and Effect Activity 5

For each item on this page, the reason something happened or how something will turn out is implied. Carefully examine each item for key words or phrases that will help you infer the cause and effect.

1 The knife Carmen was using to slice the bread was very sharp. She was surprised when drops of blood fell on the cutting board.
   a. What caused this to happen?
   b. Which key words give you clues to the cause?
   c. How will Carmen's blood affect the bread she was cutting?

2 Morty had just put the last of the books on the shelf, when suddenly it collapsed.
   a. What caused this to happen?
   b. Which key words give you clues to the cause?
   c. How might the collapse affect Morty's work schedule?

3 Gary made a large pot of chili for his friends who were coming to watch the Super Bowl. Hardly any of the chili was eaten.
   a. What caused this to happen?
   b. Which key words give you clues to the cause?
   c. How might this affect Gary's chili making in the future?

4 Sophie added a long column of numbers over and over again on her little pocket calculator. She was becoming very frustrated, because each time she came up with a different total.
   a. What caused this to happen?
   b. Which key words give you clues to the cause?
   c. How might this affect Sophie's attitude towards calculators?

5 Elaine was told about the party at the last minute because she had just returned from vacation. She arrived at the party in her red velvet dress. Everyone else was wearing jeans. She was very embarrassed.
   a. What caused this to happen?
   b. Which key words give you clues to the cause?
   c. How might this affect Elaine's experience at the party?

BETWEEN THE LINES

Answer Key

These answers are merely suggestions. The facilitator should judge if the individual's responses are appropriate for each item.

Cause and Effect Activity 1 (page 91)

1. a. Flooding, probably caused by too much rain, made the river rise.
   b. houses near the river, water in their basements
   c. The furniture and carpet will be ruined.

2. a. The cookies started to burn and smoke filled the room.
   b. cookies baking, smoke detector went off
   c. It will smell like smoke for a while. She may need to open the windows.

3. a. Skipper came in from out-of-doors with muddy paws.
   b. muddy paw prints
   c. The owner will need to take time to clean up the mess.

4. a. She didn't like the way her hair looked and wanted to get it cut, styled, or colored.
   b. looked in the mirror, then called the hairdresser
   c. She might feel good about her new look and feel more confident. She might feel like she made a mistake.

Cause and Effect Activity 2 (page 92)

1. a. The lawn mower's blades got dull from use, or Tim was tired and did a sloppy job.
   b. mowed lawns all day, last lawn
   c. People might see the last jobs and not call him for work.

2. a. A strong wind probably blew the leaves around.
   b. before lunch, when her dad got home from work (it was probably many hours later), scolded her
   c. She may bag the leaves as soon as she is done raking them next time.

3. a. The trip was cancelled because June or Benjamin became ill, or a family problem cropped up.
   b. paid for the trip; sadly, they ended up staying home
   c. They may not plan so far ahead next time.

4. a. She didn't know how to spell the word, or she needed her glasses to see the words.
   b. needed to look up a word in the dictionary, couldn't seem to find the word
   c. She may not try to use the dictionary. She may ask a parent or use a spell checker.

Section 9: Cause and Effect Inferences

5. a. He fell while skiing and broke his leg.
   b. skiing, cast on his left leg
   c. He may need help carrying things. He may need help with steps.

Cause and Effect Activity 3 (page 93)

1. a. Irene probably took her medicine twice, causing an overdose reaction.
   b. couldn't remember whether she took her medication, decided to take it before lunch, ended up in the hospital
   c. It may create serious, long-lasting health problems.

2. a. The person they had asked to water the houseplants had not done so.
   b. spent three glorious weeks on a cruise; they returned home; houseplants were withered and dying
   c. They may all die.

3. a. He was called into the treatment room, or someone ripped out the page on which the article was continued.
   b. waiting room, dentist's office, starting reading, not able to finish
   c. He may be thinking about the article and not focus on his work.

4. a. The cat jumped up on the counter where the glasses were placed and knocked them over.
   b. felt her cat, as she dried the crystal glasses, phone rang; heard the sound of breaking glass
   c. She may need to buy more glasses because now she may not have enough.

5. a. Jordan heard the familiar tune and wanted to get some ice cream.
   b. ice cream truck, playing its usual melodic tune
   c. He may be tired and cranky.

Cause and Effect Activity 4 (page 94)

1. a. He probably hit the container of juice when he took a practice swing with his bat.
   b. orange juice, practice swing with his bat, kitchen, juice, all over the kitchen floor
   c. He may be running late now because he had to clean up the juice.

2. a. The babysitter did not show up.
   b. late for work; had to ask her next-door neighbor to come and watch her baby
   c. She may be distracted because she is worried about her child. Her boss may be upset because she was late for work.

BETWEEN THE LINES

3. a. He finished quickly because he was so well prepared.
   b. studied for days, first to leave the room
   c. He will probably do well on his test.

4. a. She forgot to put film in the camera, or the batteries were dead.
   b. glad she remembered to bring her camera, ended up with no pictures
   c. She may forget parts because she doesn't have pictures to remind her.

5. a. He probably didn't speak English well enough to be understood.
   b. just arrived from Moscow, first trip to the United States, no one was able to help him
   c. He may not like it because he can't talk with the people in the United States.

Cause and Effect Activity 5 (page 95)

1. a. Without realizing it, she cut herself.
   b. knife, was very sharp, drops of blood fell
   c. She will need to throw it away.

2. a. The weight of all the books on the shelf was too great.
   b. just put the last of the books on the shelf, suddenly collapsed
   c. He will fall behind because now he needs to clean up the mess.

3. a. The chili was too spicy, everyone had eaten before they came, or someone accidentally spilled the pot of chili when it was put on the table.
   b. hardly any of the chili was eaten
   c. He may make less or make it less spicy.

4. a. The buttons are very close together on a small calculator. Sophie was hitting the wrong buttons.
   b. long column of numbers, little pocket calculator, each time she came up with a different total
   c. She may not like using calculators, or she may learn to be more careful with the buttons.

5. a. No one thought to tell her the dress code for the party.
   b. told about the party at the last minute, just returned from vacation
   c. She may feel uncomfortable and not have a good time.

Section 10: Problem/Solution Inferences

Warm-Ups

Before using the activity pages in this section, use the following warm-ups to teach the concept of problem/solution inferences.

Problem/Solution Think Alouds

Copy the *Problem/Solution Think Aloud Situations* provided in Appendix J on page 181. Read the situations and model the Think Aloud technique described on page 14. This will enable students to examine a problem and infer what the most appropriate solution would be. This requires considering all clues available in the statement, and drawing upon personal and world knowledge. Discuss the following example with the individual or group.

> **Situation**
> My best friend just told me she took a magazine from the local bookstore when the owner was not looking. Now she feels guilty about stealing, but she doesn't know what to do.
>
> **Possible Think Alouds**
> *She feels guilty, so she realizes she did a bad thing.*
>
> *She probably knows the owner, since it's a local store.*
>
> *It would be very embarrassing for her to go into the store and say, "I took this book, and I want to return it."*
>
> *One way to return the magazine would be to say to the owner, "When I left the store I didn't realize I was still holding this magazine. I'd like to return it to you."*
>
> *Even if the owner guesses what really happened, he might be inclined to forgive her and accept the ruse, since she returned it on her own after a short time.*

Use the Think Aloud technique as the situations provided in Appendix J are discussed with students. Encourage students to add their own Think Alouds as they become more comfortable with this technique.

Help Is on the Way

Copy the *Help Is on the Way* statements in Appendix J on page 182. Divide students into groups (three to four students in each group). Explain that you will be reading a list of situations that could have several different solutions. Direct students to write down as many solutions as possible, giving a minute or two for each situation. Give teams a point for each of their appropriate responses. Continue play as time allows. The team with the most points at the end wins. For example:

What would you do if you lost your lunch money?

1. *Have no lunch.*
2. *Borrow money from a friend.*
3. *Share a friend's lunch.*

Dear Abby

Collect copies of advice columns such as "Dear Abby." Discuss the solutions suggested by the columnists, as well as other solutions suggested by the members of a group. Talk about the ramifications of following through on each suggested solution.

Follow-Up Discussion

Following the above activities, explain that often in a conversation or in a reading a problem is discussed but a solution is not given. It is important to assess problems and think of a variety of appropriate solutions. There is never just one solution to a problem. However, it is important to infer what the possible ramifications of each solution could be in order to make the best decision possible. Remind students that they have now learned ways to figure out appropriate solutions to given problems. Explain that they will now have opportunities to practice this skill with the provided *Problem/Solution Activity* pages.

Remember

Before using the activity pages in this section, scan the items to determine vocabulary or world knowledge that might be unfamiliar or confusing to students. Discuss these concepts before working on the inferencing activity pages. However, be careful not to inadvertently provide too much information, taking away from the individual's opportunity to figure out new word(s) or world knowledge independently.

Section 10: Problem/Solution Inferences

NAME:_____ DATE:_____

Directions—Problem/Solution Activity 1

For each item on this page, a problem is described. Carefully examine each item and try to infer an appropriate solution. Let's look at the example.

Example

Chloe had a terrible pain on her right side below her stomach. The pain would not go away. She also had a high fever.

   a. What may be Chloe's problem? *(She may be having an appendicitis attack.)*
   b. What could Chloe do about this problem? *(She could call the doctor or go to the emergency room.)*

---

1 Four-year-old Joey was playing ball in front of his house. The ball kept rolling into the street, and Joey would run after it.

   a. What was the problem?
   b. What could Joey's parent do?

2 Hannah was staying on the 21st floor of a resort hotel. Frequently, when she went into the elevator, young children would push every button, causing the elevator to stop at every floor. Consequently, she had to waste an inordinate amount of time in the elevator.

   a. What was Hannah's problem?
   b. What could Hannah do?
   c. What could the hotel management do?

3 Gwen's friend Alicia has started to call her three or four times a day. Gwen works at home, so Alicia's calls are often an unwanted interruption. Alicia is probably lonely and just wants to chat. Gwen likes Alicia and would hate to hurt her feelings.

   a. What is Gwen's problem?
   b. What could Gwen do?

4 The last time Felix went roller-skating he fell and skinned both knees. His mother refuses to let him go roller-skating again.

   a. What is Felix's problem?
   b. What could he do about this problem?
   c. What could his mother do?

BETWEEN THE LINES

NAME:_____ DATE:_____

Directions—Problem/Solution Activity 2

For each item on this page, a problem is described. Carefully examine each item and try to infer an appropriate solution.

1. Oscar's room was a mess. His mom said he would be grounded if he didn't clean it right away. Oscar hadn't finished his homework, and he hadn't even started working on his school project.

   a. What is Oscar's problem?
   b. What could he do about this problem?
   c. What could his mother do?

2. Every year Marilyn's family would go to the seashore for summer vacation. They always had to worry because Marilyn couldn't swim.

   a. What is the problem?
   b. What could her family do about this problem?

3. Desi has trouble seeing the chalkboard when he is in the back of the room. He's afraid he may need glasses, and he doesn't think he would look good in them.

   a. What is Desi's problem?
   b. What could Desi do?
   c. What could the optometrist do?

4. Annie is starting first grade. She refuses to go if either of her parents accompanies her on her walk to school. She has to cross two intersections before she reaches the school.

   a. What is Annie's problem?
   b. What could Annie do?
   c. What could Annie's parents do?

5. Allison has a cell phone. Whenever she goes anywhere with her friend Beth, she gets calls every half hour from Beth's mother asking where they are, what they are doing, and if everything is alright. Allison finds this very annoying.

   a. What is Allison's problem?
   b. What could Allison do?
   c. What could Beth do?

Section 10: Problem/Solution Inferences

NAME:_____ DATE:_____

Directions—Problem/Solution Activity 3

For each item on this page, a problem is described. Carefully examine each item and try to infer an appropriate solution.

1 Leonardo's Dad got a new job in another city. When they move, Leonardo will have to leave his old friends behind and go to a new school. He is very unhappy.

    a. What is Leonardo's problem?
    b. What could Leonardo do?
    c. What could his parents do?

2 Peggy really likes a boy in her class. He says, "Hi" to her, but that's about all. She would like to do something to get him to notice her.

    a. What is Peggy's problem?
    b. What could Peggy do?
    c. What if Peggy's efforts fail?

3 Chelsea's sister was expecting a baby. Chelsea decided to invite a few of her sister's friends to her home for a baby shower. There was a stack of books sitting on the coffee table. After the shower, she noticed several of the books were missing.

    a. What is Chelsea's problem?
    b. What could Chelsea do?

4 Aaron's good friend was an orthodontist. When Aaron's son needed to have braces put on his teeth, he was reluctant to take him to his friend because he had heard some negative comments about his work.

    a. What is Aaron's problem?
    b. What could Aaron do?

5 Candice was happy and proud that her article had been published in a well-known professional journal. She mentioned it to a colleague and felt awful when he said, "Oh, I used to read that journal, but I don't now. The quality of the articles isn't very good anymore."

    a. What is Candice's problem?
    b. What could she do?

BETWEEN THE LINES

NAME:_____ DATE:_____

| Directions—Problem/Solution Activity 4 |

For each item on this page, a problem is described. Carefully examine each item and try to infer an appropriate solution.

1. The Baker family was enjoying dinner at a restaurant. One of the people at the next table started talking in a loud voice, and made comments that were inappropriate for children's ears.

   a. What is the Bakers' problem?
   b. What could Mr. and Mrs. Baker do?
   c. What if their efforts fail?

2. Sammy loves to go to the movies. The price of a movie ticket is $9.00. However, Sammy's allowance is only $3.00 a week.

   a. What is Sammy's problem?
   b. What could Sammy do?

3. Rita had been taking piano lessons for a year. She was considering quitting because she didn't think her piano playing was any good.

   a. What is Rita's problem?
   b. What could she do about this problem?

4. Lenny answered the phone when John called. Without her permission, Lenny accepted a date for his sister, Deidre. She didn't want to go out with John, and didn't know what to do. John would be coming to pick her up at eight o'clock on Friday night.

   a. What is Deidre's problem?
   b. What could Deidre do?
   c. What could John do?

5. The snowstorm couldn't have come at a worse time. Abby and Joe's wedding was scheduled for five o'clock. The caterer was preparing dinner for two hundred guests. Unfortunately, only those guests who lived locally would be able to make it to the wedding.

   a. What was Joe and Abby's problem?
   b. What could Abby and Joe do?

Section 10: Problem/Solution Inferences

Answer Key

These answers are merely suggestions. The facilitator should judge if the individual's responses are appropriate for each item.

Problem/Solution Activity 1 (page 101)

1. a. Joey could be hit by a vehicle if he runs into the street.
   b. Joey's mom could take away the ball, have Joey play somewhere safer, or tell Joey to call her if the ball goes into the street.

2. a. She was frustrated with children on the elevator pushing all the buttons.
   b. Hannah could try to block the children's access to the buttons by standing close to them and asking which floor they want. She could speak to the manager and ask for his or her help.
   c. The manager of the hotel could contact the parents of the children and ask them to ride the elevators with their children.

3. a. Her friend is calling her often when she is trying to get work done.
   b. Gwen could be honest with Alicia and tell her that she is working and will call her back at a more convenient time. She might let an answering machine take her calls, and then return them when she wishes.

4. a. His mother won't let him go roller-skating because she is worried he will get hurt.
   b. Felix could assure his mother that he will not go roller-skating without proper protection.
   c. His mother could let him skate in a safe area while wearing a helmet, knee pads, and elbow guards.

Problem/Solution Activity 2 (page 102)

1. a. Oscar has too many tasks that need to be finished.
   b. Oscar could talk to his mother about his need to finish his school work. He could assure her that he will clean his room on a specific day that is mutually agreeable to both of them.
   c. Once Oscar's mother realizes his problem, she could give him the opportunity to clean his room on the agreed-upon day. If he doesn't honor his promise, she could ground him.

2. a. Since she can't swim, Marilyn could drown if a wave knocks her down or an undercurrent pulls her further from the shore.
   b. Her parents could make sure Marilyn takes swimming lessons, or they could find another place to vacation where being unable to swim will not be a problem.

BETWEEN THE LINES

3. a. He can't see very well, but he doesn't want to wear glasses.
   b. Desi could have his eyes examined, deciding vision is more important than vanity.
   c. If he does need glasses, the optometrist could suggest Desi try on some frames that flatter his face, or he could suggest Desi try contact lenses.

4. a. Annie wants to walk to school alone, but her parents are worried about her safety.
   b. Annie could see if she could walk to school with other, older children.
   c. Her parents could see if there are other, older children in the neighborhood she could walk to school with, or, if the intersections are not particularly dangerous, follow Annie and see if she obeys all safety rules. A third option is for her parents to ignore her protestations and go with her to make sure she gets there safely.

5. a. Allison doesn't like getting calls from Beth's mother.
   b. Allison could either turn off her cell phone or leave it at home.
   c. Beth could assure her mother that she can be trusted to act responsibly when she is out of her sight.

Problem/Solution Activity 3 (page 103)

1. a. Leonardo doesn't want to move.
   b. Leonardo could try to be optimistic. He will probably find other children in his neighborhood or in his class he would like to have as friends.
   c. His parents could suggest he get involved in school clubs or sports as a way of meeting other children. Also, they could make an effort to meet neighbors who are likely to have children.

2. a. Peggy likes a boy, but she doesn't know if he likes her.
   b. Peggy could send him a note complimenting him on something that he did (perhaps in class or in sports) and see if he responds. She could invite him to do something with her, such as working on a school project or bike riding.
   c. If he doesn't react favorably, Peggy should forget him and reconsider the other boys in her school.

3. a. Chelsea thinks someone at the shower took some of her books.
   b. Chelsea could call the people that were at the shower and ask if, perhaps, they inadvertently forgot to put the books back on the coffee table.

4. a. Aaron doesn't want to take his son to his friend, an orthodontist, because he has heard negative things about his work. He's afraid of hurting his friend's feelings.
   b. Aaron could take his son to the best orthodontist available. Aaron might ward off any hard feelings his friend might have by telling him that he makes it a policy never to have business dealings with friends or relatives. He could investigate the negative comments made about his friend. If the comments are not true, he could have his son become his friend's orthodontic patient.

Section 10: Problem/Solution Inferences

5. a. Candice wanted the acknowledgment of a professional colleague. She was made to feel that her article was nothing special, since the journal that published it was not considered by her colleague to be good.
   b. She could just overlook the comment and chalk it up to jealousy.

Problem/Solution Activity 4 (page 104)

1. a. Their meal at a restaurant is being disrupted by others.
   b. The Bakers could ask the manager to move them to a different table. If this is not possible, the manager might, in a diplomatic manner, ask the loud individual to lower his voice and point out that young children were in the vicinity.
   c. The family could ask the server to wrap the remainder of their meals, and then eat them at home.

2. a. Sammy can't afford to go to the movies very often, so he misses many films he'd like to see.
   b. Sammy could find a way to earn money if he wants to go to the movies. He could earn money by mowing a lawn, shoveling snow, running errands, delivering newspapers, etc.

3. a. Rita is not finding her piano lessons satisfying. She doesn't think she is playing as well as she should be.
   b. She could ask her teacher how she is doing. She may be expecting too much of herself.

4. a. She has an unwanted date scheduled with John.
   b. Deidre could be a good sport and go out with John the one time so his feelings would not be hurt. She also could call him back and tell him that her brother was unaware that she already has plans for that evening. If John persists, she could explain that she thinks of him as a friend and is not interested in dating him.
   c. He could call Deidre to confirm the date, given that he never actually spoke to her.

5. a. Their wedding was during a snowstorm, and many of their guests couldn't get there.
   b. Since the wedding food was already prepared and paid for, they could call all the local people who were invited and tell them to bring their families.

Section 11: Proverbs

Background Information

A proverb is an expression that provides a moral lesson, a bit of advice on how to act or think. Like idioms, they can be taken literally or figuratively. Knowledge of proverbs is important because proverbs reflect the beliefs and values of one's society. They expand individuals' world knowledge of the society in which they live.

Proverbs, according to the "meta semantic hypothesis," are learned through an active analysis of the words they contain (Nippold, Allen, & Kirsch, 2001). This contrasts with the view that they are learned holistically, as large units, where proverb comprehension reflects the use of rote memory rather than constructive mental activity (Honeck, Voegtle, Dorfmueller, & Hoffman, 1980).

While knowing key words may promote understanding for some proverbs, others may remain obscure until analyzed from other perspectives (e.g., contextual information). The proverbs in *Between the Lines* were selected from those often found in textbooks, other media, and spontaneous conversational interactions.

Let's Practice Proverbs

Discuss with students that a proverb is a figure of speech that generally gives advice or teaches a lesson. Often, the meaning of a proverb can be figured out by examining what the words appear to be saying. Look before you leap, for example, seems to be saying, be careful and don't do something without considering the consequences. Sometimes the meaning is not so obvious. For example, the proverb A little knowledge is a dangerous thing may be confusing unless it is thought through very carefully. Following is an example discussion you may have with individuals relating to this proverb.

> *In what situation might knowing only a little bit about something be dangerous? Is there a time when you only knew a little bit about something and it caused a problem? Many times when students in medical school are learning about a disease, for example, they think they have it. They may have some of the symptoms, but do not have enough information to consider these symptoms accurately or appropriately. They don't know enough to realize that the symptoms can be typical of many other medical problems, or that they may be of little or no importance.*

Proverbs are figurative expressions and are not meant to be taken literally. For example, He who laughs last, laughs best means a person should go ahead with what he is doing and not worry when others laugh at him. When he succeeds, he will enjoy laughing at them for being wrong more than they enjoyed laughing at him. If taken literally it would mean the person who laughs after everyone else has laughed, has the best laugh.

Between the Lines

Mention to individuals that a multiple-choice format is used in this section. Each item has three statements. At least one, or possibly two or three, of the statements illustrate the proverb's meaning. Advise students that proverbs are not to be taken in their literal sense. Some proverbs are rather opaque, and their meaning is not readily apparent from the words that compose them. If the statements themselves are insufficient for drawing out the meaning of the proverb, guiding questions, followed by in-depth discussion of possible responses, can help reveal the proverb's meaning. Let's look at the examples.

Example 1

Evan was not playing well and was losing his tennis match. He ran for a long shot and sprained his ankle. He limped home slowly and tripped over a rock in the road, spraining the other ankle. <u>When it rains it pours</u>.

A. Which statement(s) best tell(s) the meaning of the proverb? *(a and c)*
   a. The same day John got a big promotion, he won the state Lottery.
   b. April showers are responsible for May flowers.
   c. Mom was sick with the flu, Timmy had an earache, and Dad's car broke down.

B. Taking the statement(s) selected into consideration, what does the proverb mean? *(A lot of good things, or bad things, may happen at the same time.)*

C. Describe a time when you could have used this proverb.

Example 2

Marcia and Steve had just gotten engaged. They were talking about when and where they would have their wedding when Steve's friend John rang the doorbell. They both thought, "<u>Two's company, three's a crowd</u>."

A. Which statement(s) best tell(s) the meaning of the proverb? *(c)*
   a. Our dining room always seems crowded when we invite more than three people for dinner.
   b. The Clarks were happy when Tess Harper came to see them.
   c. Hope and Hank were cuddling next to the fire when the doorbell rang and spoiled everything.

B. Taking the statement(s) selected into consideration, what does the proverb mean? *(When two people want to be alone with each other and a third, uninvited person comes to join them, the uninvited person is unwelcome.)*

C. Describe a time when you could have used this proverb.

Section 11: Proverbs

NAME:_____ DATE:_____

Directions—Proverbs Activity 1

Look at the proverbs on these two pages and carefully examine the statements below each one. For question A, use your inferencing skills to select the statement(s) that best tell(s) the meaning of each of the underlined proverbs. Then answers questions B and C.

1 Daisy gave Joanne an expensive sweater for her birthday. Although the sweater fit nicely, Joanne would have chosen a different color. Her mother said, "Don't look a gift horse in the mouth."

    A. Which statement(s) best tell(s) the meaning of the proverb?

        a. Manny didn't like the hubcaps on the car his uncle gave him, but Dad said he shouldn't complain.

        b. Joe tried to see if the horse had all its teeth.

        c. Maria thought that getting a horse for her birthday was wonderful, and she looked it over carefully.

    B. Taking the statement(s) selected into consideration, what does the proverb mean?

    C. Describe a time when you could have used this proverb.

2 Don't hang out with Tina and Rochelle. They never study and frequently cut classes. Remember, people think, "Birds of a feather flock together."

    A. Which statement(s) best tell(s) the meaning of the proverb?

        a. All the "brains" joined the chess club.

        b. Bernie's reputation suffered when he become friendly with the boys who pushed other kids around.

        c. You can usually find all of the birds in one section of the zoo.

    B. Taking the statement(s) selected into consideration, what does the proverb mean?

    C. Describe a time when you could have used this proverb.

BETWEEN THE LINES

3. Jeremy and Amanda were going on vacation. There had been some robberies in town, so Amanda was going to put her jewelry into a safe deposit box at the bank. She was so busy she forgot to go to the bank. When they came home, their house had been broken into and her jewelry was gone. Amanda cried and cried. Jeremy said, "<u>You can't lock the barn door after the horse is stolen</u>."

   A. Which statement(s) best tell(s) the meaning of the proverb?
      a. Animals can't lock the door by themselves.
      b. Leonard failed his math test and decided he should have spent more time studying.
      c. When Caroline came out of her house and didn't see her car in the driveway, she realized that she shouldn't have left the keys in the ignition.
   B. Taking the statement(s) selected into consideration, what does the proverb mean?
   C. Describe a time when you could have used this proverb.

4. Sometimes we forget that the kids are in the room when we have our "adults only" discussions. We have to remember that, <u>little pitchers have big ears</u>.

   A. Which statement(s) best tell(s) the meaning of the proverb?
      a. Jessie, it's not a good idea to talk about our neighbors in front of the children.
      b. Ronnie was upset when his little league teammates teased him because his ears stuck out.
      c. Even small pitchers can have large handles.
   B. Taking the statement(s) selected into consideration, what does the proverb mean?
   C. Describe a time when you could have used this proverb.

Section 11: Proverbs

NAME:_____ DATE:_____

Directions—Proverbs Activity 2

Look at the proverbs on these two pages and carefully examine the statements below each one. For question A, use your inferencing skills to select the statement(s) that best tell(s) the meaning of each of the underlined proverbs. Then answer questions B and C.

 "When I grow up," said Nancy, "I would like to be a pilot. But I'm worried about whether I'll be able to learn how to take off and land the plane safely, and how to navigate." Her mom said, "Don't cross your bridges until you come to them."

    A. Which statement(s) best tell(s) the meaning of the proverb?

        a. It's a good idea to get a road map before embarking on a long trip.
        b. Why don't you wait and see if you got the part in the play before you decide you won't be able to memorize the lines.
        c. Stop and think before you go across a bridge.

    B. Taking the statement(s) selected into consideration, what does the proverb mean?

    C. Describe a time when you could have used this proverb.

When Jim went shopping with his dad, he thought he would get a new pair of running shoes and winter boots. His dad only bought the boots. Oh well, thought Jim, "Half a loaf is better than none."

    A. Which statement(s) best tell(s) the meaning of the proverb?

        a. Patti earned much less than she expected for babysitting all summer, but at least she earned enough to pay for her college textbooks.
        b. The bakery decided it would be good business to sell half loaves of bread for small families.
        c. So what if she only gave you three candies, something is better than nothing.

    B. Taking the statement(s) selected into consideration, what does the proverb mean?

    C. Describe a time when you could have used this proverb.

Between the Lines

3 Stella uses the phone more than anyone in the family. Her brother Peter made two calls in a row, and Stella ran to tell her mother. Peter said, "People who live in glass houses shouldn't throw stones."

  A. Which statement(s) best tell(s) the meaning of the proverb?
   a. Gloria complains about Jennifer's habit of spreading vicious rumors, but Gloria does it more than anyone else.
   b. There was an enormous amount of breakage in Terry's house.
   c. Joe was not well liked, so people thought it was okay to toss rocks through the windows of his house.

  B. Taking the statement(s) selected into consideration, what does the proverb mean?

  C. Describe a time when you could have used this proverb.

4 Jessica always promises to help with the dishes, but somehow she never does. I say, "Actions speak louder than words."

  A. Which statement(s) best tell(s) the meaning of the proverb?
   a. Zelda had to shout for five minutes before Frank would turn off his stereo.
   b. For weeks Edward has been promising to paint my room, but he still hasn't gotten around to it.
   c. A good mime has no need for words.

  B. Taking the statement(s) selected into consideration, what does the proverb mean?

  C. Describe a time when you could have used this proverb.

Section 11: Proverbs

NAME:_____ DATE:_____

| Directions—Proverbs Activity 3 |

Look at the proverbs on these two pages and carefully examine the statements below each one. For question A, use your inferencing skills to select the statement(s) that best tell(s) the meaning of each of the underlined proverbs. Then answer questions B and C.

1 Even though Jackie is sometimes thoughtless, she comes through when you really need her. <u>A friend in need is a friend indeed</u>.

    A. Which statement(s) best tell(s) the meaning of the proverb?

        a. When I needed a ride to the hospital in the middle of the night, I knew I could count on Grace.

        b. When Mario's house was flooded by the rising river, Julius asked Mario and his family to stay at his house until the water subsided and repairs were made.

        c. Harriet stayed all evening to help me study for the math quiz I had to take in the morning.

    B. Taking the statement(s) selected into consideration, what does the proverb mean?

    C. Describe a time when you could have used this proverb.

2 You've been working on that project all day. You haven't had time to think of anything else. Take a break. Go out and have some fun! <u>All work and no play makes Jack a dull boy</u>.

    A. Which statement(s) best tell(s) the meaning of the proverb?

        a. Marc is not very smart because he never plays with the other children.

        b. Working all the time will help you get ahead.

        c. The doctor told Mr. James to stop working on weekends and start playing golf, tennis, or baseball.

    B. Taking the statement(s) selected into consideration, what does the proverb mean?

    C. Describe a time when you could have used this proverb.

BETWEEN THE LINES

3 Marianne loved to go to the movies, but she refused to go with Toby because she was mad at him. Toby said, "<u>Don't cut off your nose to spite your face</u>."

   A. Which statement(s) best tell(s) the meaning of the proverb?

   a. Jonathan refused to eat his favorite dinner because his mother made him clean his room before coming to the table.

   b. Gretchen decided to go to a plastic surgeon to have her nose made smaller.

   c. Becca was happy when Anne said she didn't want to go to the movies on Saturday.

   B. Taking the statement(s) selected into consideration, what does the proverb mean?

   C. Describe a time when you could have used this proverb.

4 Eva wanted to know everything and was always asking one question after another. At times she asked rather personal questions. Her mother said, "You don't have to know everything, Eva. Remember, <u>curiosity killed the cat</u>."

   A. Which statement(s) best tell(s) the meaning of the proverb?

   a. Just before Christmas, Frank was searching all the closets in the house, hoping to come across hidden presents.

   b. "Mind your own business or you'll be in big trouble" said Nona's big sister.

   c. "Don't ask so many questions, Judy. You'll find out about our vacation plans in due course."

   B. Taking the statement(s) selected into consideration, what does the proverb mean?

   C. Describe a time when you could have used this proverb.

Section 11: Proverbs

NAME:_____ DATE:_____

Directions—Proverbs Activity 4

Look at the proverbs on these two pages and carefully examine the statements below each one. For question A, use your inferencing skills to select the statement(s) that best tell(s) the meaning of each of the underlined proverbs. Then answer questions B and C.

1 After the graduation party, the house was a horrible mess. Rosie needed to get the house cleaned. She couldn't decide whether to draft members of her family to help her or hire a cleaning service. She'd do whatever it took as long as the job was done. After all, <u>all roads lead to Rome</u>.

    A. Which statement(s) best tell(s) the meaning of the proverb?

        a. After they wrote out the invitations, it was all systems go for the wedding.

        b. "I don't care how you get the answers," said Audrey's teacher. "Use the encyclopedia, the Internet, or your textbooks. Just make sure you have them by tomorrow."

        c. All of a sudden, the ship hit an iceberg. The captain told the first mate to sound the "abandon ship" alarm.

    B. Taking the statement(s) selected into consideration, what does the proverb mean?

    C. Describe a time when you could have used this proverb.

2 Jim was very taken with the black car in the used car lot. The paint finish was like new, and the interior was beautiful. He decided to take it out for a test drive. What a dud! It stalled twice in five minutes and chugged slowly uphill. It just goes to show, <u>all that glitters is not gold</u>.

    A. Which statement(s) best tell(s) the meaning of the proverb?

        a. Cherie thought the bracelet was beautiful. It had so many sparkling stones. When she showed it to her mother, she was told that it was costume jewelry, and not very valuable.

        b. Father drove a hard bargain with the real estate agent when we bought our new home.

        c. Many beautiful women go to Hollywood to become movie stars. Few of them actually reach the top.

BETWEEN THE LINES

   B. Taking the statement(s) selected into consideration, what does the proverb mean?

   C. Describe a time when you could have used this proverb.

3 Grandpa said, "I can't take up oil painting at my age. After all, <u>you can't teach an old dog new tricks</u>."

   A. Which statement(s) best tell(s) the meaning of the proverb?
      a. Kathleen was delighted that all of her new students, from 52 to 73 years of age, had made great progress in their flute playing this year.
      b. It's interesting to note that so many people over 65 are taking computer courses.
      c. Donna tried and tried but, after 45 years of driving cars with automatic transmission, she found it very difficult to switch to a car with a stick shift.

   B. Taking the statement(s) selected into consideration, what does the proverb mean?

   C. Describe a time when you could have used this proverb.

4 Dave was very nervous about his first day of high school in September. In August he went on a vacation to Hawaii. He forgot all about school. No textbooks, notebooks, or backpack around to remind him. After all, <u>out of sight, out of mind</u>.

   A. Which statement(s) best tell(s) the meaning of the proverb?
      a. Curt was very friendly and attentive to the group of tourists he took up in his helicopter. When their ride was over, he transferred all of his attention to the next group.
      b. When Becca's dad got a job in another state she was very sad. She had to move away from her best friend, Rachel. She promised she would always write, call, and e-mail. Thirty years later, they are still in touch, and visiting each other at least once every year.
      c. Harry was very unhappy when his girlfriend, Annie, no longer wanted to go out with him. Three weeks later he started to date Jane, and Annie became a vague memory.

   B. Taking the statement(s) selected into consideration, what does the proverb mean?

   C. Describe a time when you could have used this proverb.

Section 11: Proverbs

Answer Key

These answers are merely suggestions. The facilitator should judge if the individual's responses are appropriate for each item. Note that since letter c responses are individual to each student, no suggestions are given.

Proverbs Activity 1 (pages 111–112)

1. A. a
   B. Don't complain when a gift is not perfect.

2. A. a and b
   B. People of the same type often seem to gather together. If you are often with certain people, you may be considered to be like them.

3. A. b and c
   B. Don't wait to do something until it is too late.

4. A. a
   B. Little children often overhear things they are not supposed to hear or things adults do not expect them to notice.

Proverbs Activity 2 (pages 113–114)

1. A. b
   B. Don't worry about future events before they happen.

2. A. a and c
   B. Getting part of what we want or need is better than getting nothing.

3. A. a
   B. Don't complain about other people if you are as bad as they are.

4. A. b
   B. What you do about something is more important than what you say you'll do.

Proverbs Activity 3 (pages 115–116)

1. A. a, b, and c
   B. A true friend is a person on whom you can always depend; a person who will help you when you really need someone.

2. A. c
   B. Too much hard work without time out for enjoyment is not good for anyone.

3. A. a
   B. Don't harm yourself in trying to punish another person.

Between the Lines

4. A. a, b, and c
   B. Getting too nosy may lead a person into trouble.

Proverbs Activity 4 (pages 117–118)

1. A. b
   B. The same end or goal may be reached by many different ways.

2. A. a
   B. Many attractive and alluring things have little or no value.

3. A. c
   B. It is very hard or almost impossible to train an older person to acquire a new skill.

4. A. a and c
   B. If you do not see something, you will not think about it.

Section 12: Paragraph Analysis

Background Information

Analyzing paragraphs calls into play the highest levels of thinking skills (i.e., analysis, synthesis, and evaluation). Wallach and Lee (1982) and Wallach and Lee-Schachter (1984) found paragraph analysis to be an effective way to improve inferencing skills. In this section the individual has to determine which sentence in a paragraph is tangential to the topic being discussed and synthesize a more appropriate replacement sentence.

Let's Practice Paragraph Analysis

Copy the *Paragraph Analysis Story Webs* in Appendix K on pages 183–184. The first web is completed for you to correlate with the first example below. The other web is blank. The facilitator is encouraged to use copies of the blank web when working with students throughout the *Paragraph Analysis Activity* pages. This section is composed of short paragraphs. All of the sentences, except one, belong to the same topic. Direct students to use their inferencing skills to find the sentence that does not belong, and replace it with a more appropriate sentence. Note that the sentence that does not belong is often closely related to the topic, so careful analysis is required. Let's look at the examples:

Example 1

Lee was dedicated to her ice skating practice. She practiced figure eights and quick turns for five hours before leaving the ice. Spins were on her agenda for the next day. Her outfit was blue and white. If she continued to practice every day, she would have a good chance at winning the gold medal.

Delete: *Her outfit was blue and white.*
Replace with: *She was very systematic in her efforts to reach her goal.*

Example 2

I really love parades. Our town wanted to do something special to honor war veterans on Memorial Day. The mayor decided to form a program committee. The committee members decided to ask three of the town's leading citizens to give speeches. All three had served in the military. The entire population of the town turned out to hear their speeches.

Delete: *I really love parades.*
Replace with: *It was May, and Memorial Day falls at the end of the month.*

BETWEEN THE LINES

NAME:_____ DATE:_____

Directions—Paragraph Activity 1

Read each paragraph on this page. All of the sentences, except one, belong to the same topic. Use your inferencing skills to find the sentence that does not belong. Underline this sentence and then replace it with a more appropriate sentence. Note that the sentence that does not belong is often closely related to the topic, so careful analysis is required.

1. The birthday party is tomorrow. Beth started decorating the house with balloons and signs. She hung strips of colorful crepe paper. Rose helped her pick out the birthday cake. The balloons will burst if someone pokes them with a pin.

_____

2. The orchestra still needed two more oboe players and a flutist before the next concert season began. Wendy decided to audition for the flute position. Her audition went very well. There were many woodwind instruments. After the audition, the orchestra leader said, "Now we only need two oboe players."

_____

3. Each child was sitting quietly, waiting for the test to begin. Everyone's nerves were on edge because the test was the most important one of the school year. The weather was hot and humid. Everyone's pencils were sharpened. The test would take about three hours.

_____

4. The meteorologist was predicting a storm. The sky was dark, and storm clouds thickly covered the area. Last time the sky looked this way we had a torrential downpour. After a storm, I love it when there's a rainbow. I hope the streets don't get flooded again.

_____

Section 12: Paragraph Analysis

NAME:_____ DATE:_____

| Directions—Paragraph Activity 2 |

Read each paragraph on this page. All of the sentences, except one, belong to the same topic. Use your inferencing skills to find the sentence that does not belong. Underline this sentence and then replace it with a more appropriate sentence. Note that the sentence that does not belong is often closely related to the topic, so careful analysis is required.

1 Mary and John's wedding was planned for June. That left only six months to complete the arrangements. Mary needed to buy a wedding gown, and the bridesmaid dresses had to be ordered. A caterer and photographer had to be hired. More people get married in June than any other month.

_____

2 Michelle wanted a dog. She begged her mother to allow her to get a puppy from her neighbor. Her mom was reluctant because she didn't know if Michelle would take all responsibility for the dog's care. Beth and Grace had dogs. Finally, Mom decided to allow Michelle to have a puppy.

_____

3 A visit to California wouldn't be complete without a stop in San Francisco. The Cannery, Fisherman's Wharf, and Lombard Street are only a few of the interesting sights. Earthquakes are generally very mild. It's not too far to make a side trip along the Pacific Coast to see Carmel or Monterey.

_____

4 Kathleen thought growing a flower garden would be an excellent hobby. She always loved colorful flowers. Kathleen had browsed through gardening magazines to get an idea of which flowers were most appealing to her. Planting vegetables would have been more practical. When the flowers bloomed, she was excited by the beautiful splashes of color and the delightful aroma.

_____

BETWEEN THE LINES

NAME:_____ DATE:_____

Directions — Paragraph Activity 3

Read each paragraph on this page. All of the sentences, except one, belong to the same topic. Use your inferencing skills to find the sentence that does not belong. Underline this sentence and then replace it with a more appropriate sentence. Note that the sentence that does not belong is often closely related to the topic, so careful analysis is required.

1 Peter wanted to play basketball all the time. He had dreams of becoming a professional basketball player. His mom told him to study more. However, he had one problem. He was one of the shortest kids in his class. Peter hoped he would grow a lot over the next few years.

_____

2 Joyce went to the movies with Alan every Friday night. Alan loved to see action films. Occasionally they would argue because Joyce preferred to see romantic movies. They decided to alternate. Alan would pick the film one week and Joyce would pick it the next. Sometimes they would go to the show with another couple.

_____

3 Amir and Hassan loved to build and fly kites. Each spring they would go to the hobby shop and buy bamboo for the spars, thin tissue paper, glue, and string. The wind is too strong for kite flying in the wintertime. They would put a lot of time and effort into making a good kite. When they were done making their kite they would fly it at the seashore, where they could run along the sand for a long time without stopping.

_____

4 Georgia and Dan were distressed when they were told that their roof couldn't be repaired. They needed a new roof. A new roof cost more money than they had in the bank. It looked like they would have to take out a loan from the bank. It's difficult to live in a house with a leaky roof.

_____

Section 12: Paragraph Analysis

Answer Key

It is up to the individual facilitator to determine a more appropriate sentence as a replacement for the sentence that doesn't belong. The following sentences are merely examples.

Paragraph Activity 1 (page 122)

1. (The balloons will burst if someone pokes them with a pin.) Everything looked great and Beth was ready for the happy occasion.

2. (There were many woodwind instruments.) In fact, she played so well she got the job.

3. (The weather was hot and humid.) They had all studied for weeks before the test.

4. (After a storm, I love it when there's a rainbow.) I'd better make sure all the windows are closed.

Paragraph Activity 2 (page 123)

1. (More people get married in June than any other month.) They hoped that everything would be ready in time for the big event.

2. (Beth and Grace had dogs.) Michelle vowed she would feed, walk, and clean up after the dog every day.

3. (Earthquakes are generally very mild.) There are many very good restaurants in all price ranges.

4. (Planting vegetables would have been more practical.) She went to the local nursery and bought a variety of flower seeds.

Paragraph Activity 3 (page 124)

1. (His mom told him to study more.) He practiced shooting baskets every chance he got.

2. (Sometimes they would go to the show with another couple.) This turned out to be a satisfactory compromise.

3. (The wind is too strong for kite flying in the wintertime.) They hoped the kites they would make would be as good as the ones they had made the previous year.

4. (It's difficult to live in a house with a leaky roof.) Early the next morning they went to speak to the bank manager to see how quickly they could get a loan.

Section 13: Visual Humor

Background Information

The expression "a picture is worth a thousand words" makes us realize that other modalities are often more appropriate for getting our message across than the words we speak. In conversation, for example, a tone of voice or intonation pattern helps clarify the meaning of a spoken message. In the case of visual humor, what we see (i.e., the graphic representation) can be a crucial tool for accurately interpreting the text of the humor. Or, if there are no words, the picture can be a tool for interpreting the humorist's intention. We can infer, or arrive at a conclusion, by reasoning from visual evidence. Given that humor appears to foster creative thinking in both younger and older individuals (Isen, Daubman, & Nowicki, 1987; Ziv, 1988), cartoons and comic strips are an excellent source of visual material requiring inferencing skills. The humor items can be visual only (no text) or visual with text.

Let's Practice Visual Humor

For the following cartoon, it is necessary to examine the picture and the caption to figure out the basis of the humor. Explore this example with students.

"You again?"

    a. What is the basis of the humor? *(The expression, "A cat has nine lives.")*

    b. What do you see in the cartoon and caption that give you clues? *(A cat is looking at what appears to be St. Peter because he has angel's wings and a halo. He is standing by what appears to be the gates of heaven. "You again?" implies that the cat has already died at least once before, and he has lost yet another of his nine lives.)*

BETWEEN THE LINES

Directions—Visual Humor

For each item on the following pages, there is a cartoon in which the basis of its humor is implied. Carefully examine each cartoon and answer the questions that follow.

"Anyone else have an objection?"

a. What is the basis of the humor in this cartoon?

b. What do you see in the cartoon and caption that give you clues?

Section 13: Visual Humor

a. What is the basis of the humor in this cartoon?

b. What do you see in the cartoon that gives you clues?

"If I were you buddy, I'd finish the soda and get out of here."

a. What is the basis of the humor in this cartoon?

b. What do you see in the cartoon and caption that give you clues?

BETWEEN THE LINES

"How do you expect me to weigh you while you're wearing those heavy boots?"

    a. What is the basis of the humor in this cartoon?

    b. What do you see in the cartoon and caption that give you clues?

"Nobody told me this was a formal meeting."

    a. What is the basis of the humor?

    b. What do you see in the cartoon and caption that give you clues?

"On the other hand, I have a rather unusual idea."

a. What is the basis of the humor?
b. What do you see in the cartoon and caption that give you clues?

a. What is the basis of the humor?
b. What do you see in the cartoon that give you clues?

Between the Lines

"Is there a history of severe back pain in your family?"

a. What is the basis of the humor?
b. What do you see in the cartoon and caption that give you clues?

Section 13: Visual Humor

Answer Key (pages 128–132)

1. a. The humor is based on the knowledge that lions eat rabbits.
   b. There is an empty chair which was probably filled by another rabbit, and the comment, "Anyone else have an objection?" leads us to infer that the lion was displeased with and ate the rabbit that occupied the empty chair.

2. a. The man has a bandage on his rather large nose.
   b. His arms are short so we can infer that when he clashed the cymbals together, his nose got in the way and was injured.

3. a. Hammers hit nails on their heads.
   b. The hammers are looking at the nail, and the man behind the counter tells the nail it would be wise if it left quickly. We can infer that if the nail stays, it will be hit on the head by the hammers.

4. a. The man is holding his boots while he is standing on the scale.
   b. If the man holds the boots while he is on the scale, his weight will be the same as when he is wearing them. When the nurse implies that he should remove them, and he takes them off and then holds them, we can infer that he is not intelligent.

5. a. Penguins look as if they are wearing tuxedos.
   b. We can infer that the addition of a bow tie, for a penguin, indicates formal attire, as noted by the "tie-less" penguin's comment in the caption.

6. a. Rabbits like to eat carrots.
   b. Plastic surgeons often shorten and change people's noses. Since the doctor is a rabbit, we can infer that the unusual idea noted in the caption would be the rabbit altering the snowman's nose by biting off a piece of it.

7. a. The "worm's-eye" view gives the worm a false impression of what is squeezed out of a tube of toothpaste.
   b. We can infer that the worm thinks the long "squirt" of toothpaste is another worm. The hearts indicate that he has fallen in love.

8. a. The doctor is not seeing the real problem, and is, as shown in the caption, focusing on routine questions asked of a patient at a doctor's office.
   b. The patient has a large knife sticking in his back. We can infer that the doctor hasn't seen it or he would be aware that the pain is caused by the knife and not by some general problem affecting members of his family.

Section 14: "Because" Statements

Background Information

Individuals with the ability to complete "because" statements appropriately, show they have attained the highest level of thinking skills—the combined use of analysis, synthesis, and evaluation. At this level, they can use their inferencing skills to critically judge information and provide suitable endings for "because" utterances.

Let's Practice Completing "Because" Statements

Read the following items aloud. Ask students to analyze each situation and infer an appropriate conclusion to complete each statement. Just for fun, ask students to use their imagination and wit to provide "unusual" conclusions to utterances with an asterisk.

- I enjoy having flowers in my backyard…*(because they are so beautiful and have a wonderful aroma)*.

- I eat soup with a spoon…*(because if I used a fork the liquid in the soup would fall through the tines)*.

- *I like to go to the zoo…*(because then I can see an elephant on the telephant, or is it an elephone on the telephone)*.

- It's always best to put chewed gum in the trash when you're finished with it…*(because if you drop it on the ground it will stick to someone's shoe)*.

- Spending an afternoon at an aquarium is educational…*(because you see and read about a large variety of fish you'd never see anywhere else)*.

- If given a choice, I would rather write with a pencil than a pen…*(because you can't erase or make changes if you use a pen)*.

BETWEEN THE LINES

NAME:_____ DATE:_____

Directions—"Because" Activity 1

Complete the following "because" statements. If the statement has an asterisk (*) next to it, use your imagination and give it a funny or unusual ending.

1. Children should never go into a pool alone...

2. I like a sunny day better than a rainy day...

3. I wear a hat and gloves in the winter...

4. Going to a museum is interesting...

5. *I never ate green eggs and ham...

6. I take books out of the library...

7. My dad can play the piano very well...

8. Don't eat too much junk food...

9. Houses have doorbells...

10. *Watermelon is messy...

11. Mom is a good swimmer...

12. In the summertime I drink lots of water...

13. Uncle Jeff is fun...

14. *People use leashes to walk dogs...

15. I wear a watch...

16. You should always play with your friends...

Section 14: "Because" Statements

NAME:_____ DATE:_____

Directions—"Because" Activity 2

Complete the following "because" statements. If the statement has an asterisk (*) next to it, use your imagination and give it a funny or unusual ending.

1. Sometimes it's difficult to eat taffy…

2. *We wear shoes…

3. I would like to speak a foreign language…

4. I wear glasses…

5. Dad wears a suit and tie when he goes to work…

6. I love to travel…

7. People applaud at shows…

8. Pencils have erasers…

9. *I wish I could fly…

10. It's not a good idea to approach a bear cub…

11. Peter polished his shoes…

12. Never cross the street without looking both ways…

13. You should always get enough sleep…

14. I don't like mosquitoes…

15. Dentists tell people to brush their teeth twice daily…

16. Use a ruler when drawing a line…

BETWEEN THE LINES

NAME:_____ DATE:_____

Directions—"Because" Activity 3

Complete the following "because" statements. If the statement has an asterisk (*) next to it, use your imagination and give it a funny or unusual ending.

1. Many people sleep in pajamas…

2. Don't leave milk out of the refrigerator overnight…

3. Snakes crawl on the ground…

4. Tanya put on her headset…

5. It's hard not to pucker when you eat a lemon…

6. *Giraffes prefer elephants as friends…

7. Some people need to wear belts…

8. I don't eat baby food…

9. It's good to have thumbs…

10. Never stand near the sidewalk curb after a heavy rain…

11. A motorcycle can go faster than a bicycle…

12. It's not a good idea to hide alone on a wilderness trail…

13. You should not practice a musical instrument in the middle of the night…

14. *When I eat jellybeans I take one of each color, and then start again with the first color…

15. Always wear a seatbelt when riding in a car…

16. It's not a good idea to go up a down staircase…

Section 14: "Because" Statements

NAME:_____ DATE:_____

Directions—"Because" Activity 4

Complete the following "because" statements. If the statement has an asterisk (*) next to it, use your imagination and give it a funny or unusual ending.

1. Many people love a rainy day…

2. Storekeepers don't like to be paid in pennies…

3. Pillow fights are fun…

4. Many people prefer to read chapter books…

5. It's easier to put mittens on babies than gloves…

6. It's better if a tall person sits behind a shorter person in a movie theater…

7. *You should not try to make a hippopotamus sandwich…

8. An elephant can't sit on a mouse…

9. Lying on the beach for several hours may not be a good idea…

10. It's easier to eat grapes than grapefruit…

11. I'm glad pencils have erasers…

12. We eat dessert after the main part of our meal…

13. A warm coat is necessary in the winter in Alaska…

14. Judges use gavels…

15. Birthday parties are fun…

16. After you use toothpaste, put the cover back on…

BETWEEN THE LINES

Answer Key

The following responses are merely examples. The facilitator should judge if the individual's responses are appropriate for each item.

"Because" Activity 1 (page 136)
1. because they are in danger of drowning.
2. because I can play ball, garden, go bicycle riding, or go for a walk.
3. because I live in a cold part of the country, and they keep me warm.
4. because you can see objects from the past that you can't see anywhere else.
5. because Dr. Seuss's characters ate them up before I had a chance to try any.
6. because I love to read, and I can borrow different books every week.
7. because he took lessons and practiced a lot.
8. because it isn't nutritious, and you can become overweight.
9. because you need to hear if someone is at the door even if you are in another part of your home.
10. because your hair gets wet and full of seeds when you bend down to bite into it.
11. because when she was a child, she had a pool and swam every day during the summer months.
12. because the heat dehydrates me, and I need lots of fluids to stay healthy.
13. because he always has great ideas for how to spend our time.
14. because dogs like to run off and play in their friends' backyards.
15. because I need to know when it's time for lunch.
16. because it's the right thing to do.

"Because" Activity 2 (page 137)
1. because it sticks to your teeth.
2. because we don't like to look at our toes.
3. because I could speak to and understand people when I go to a country where that language is spoken.
4. because my vision is poor, and I can see better with them.
5. because he is a businessman, and that is how he is expected to dress in his office.
6. because I enjoy meeting people from different parts of the world and seeing new and interesting sights.

Section 14: "Because" Statements

7. because that is how they let the actors know how much they appreciate their talents.
8. because people make mistakes that need to be corrected.
9. because I'd never have to wait for planes at airports whenever I'd travel.
10. because its mother is probably nearby and may attack you if she thinks you are a danger to her offspring.
11. because he was going on a date with his girlfriend.
12. because you may be hit by an oncoming car or truck.
13. because it's difficult to think or act appropriately if you're tired.
14. because it itches when they bite.
15. because bacteria that causes tooth decay are formed in our mouths from eating and drinking.
16. because it will be easier to make the line straight.

"Because" Activity 3 (page 138)

1. because they are more comfortable than sleeping in other kinds of clothing.
2. because it will spoil (turn sour).
3. because they don't have legs, so they can't walk.
4. because she wanted to listen to music without disturbing anyone.
5. because it's sour.
6. *because they don't have to bend over as much to converse with them.
7. because if they didn't, their pants would fall down.
8. because I have teeth and can chew regular food, and there isn't as much flavor and variety in baby foods.
9. because thumbs work with your other fingers to enable you to manipulate things.
10. because oncoming vehicles will splash you with water from puddles in the road.
11. because it has a motor.
12. because if anything happens to you (e.g., a fall that causes injury, getting lost) no one will know, and you won't be able to get help.
13. because you would wake anyone who is nearby.
14. *because I don't want any of the jellybeans to be jealous if they're not picked.

BETWEEN THE LINES

15. because it will protect you if the car stops quickly, or if you're in an accident.
16. because you may get knocked over by people coming down.

"Because" Activity 4 (page 139)

1. because they enjoy cuddling up inside with a good book and listening to the sound of the rain.
2. because it takes too long to count them, and the pennies take up too much room in the cash drawer.
3. because you can hit someone and not hurt him or her.
4. because it's easy to read one chapter each night before going to bed.
5. because babies can't put each finger into the gloves by themselves, so an older person would have to do it.
6. because then both of them would be able to see the screen.
7. *because it's too difficult to get the hippo between the two slices of bread.
8. *because the mouse would run away quickly before the elephant would have a chance to sit down.
9. because you could get badly sunburned.
10. because you don't have to peel or cut them.
11. because they enable me to correct my mistakes.
12. because if we eat dessert first we may be full and unable to eat the more nutritious part of our meal.
13. because winters in Alaska are frigid, and you'd be very cold without one.
14. because noisy people in a courtroom will quiet down if they hear the banging sound of the gavel.
15. because you can have family and friends help you eat birthday cake and celebrate.
16. because otherwise it will dry up and be useless.

Section 15: Bridging Activities

Several of the following activities should be completed after finishing sections 1–14. These activities will help students bridge the information learned in *Between the Lines* to situations they encounter at home and in school. In this section, emphasize to students the importance of making correct inferences in their daily lives.

1. Ask individuals to make up items similar to those in the various sections of *Between the Lines*. Offer assistance, if necessary, until they can develop items on their own.

2. Explore newspapers and magazines for statements that require inferencing.

    Example
    Let's hope the Black Hawks win today. Otherwise, Coach Thompson may be job hunting.
    (Inference: *The coach may be fired if the team loses.*)

3. Check out the illustrations in magazine advertisements for inferencing possibilities. The advertising industry frequently uses implied messages as part of sales campaigns.

    Example
    A carpet company was advertising a nautical blue carpet. The illustration showed a small sailboat that looked as if it was sailing across the carpet. A broken bottle topped by a cork was shown lying on a table nearby. The caption read, "Fantastic Voyage."
    (Inference: *The ship was enticed to escape from the bottle because the carpeting was so appealing—it looked like a big blue ocean.*)

4. Have individuals discuss the key words or phrases in passages selected from level-appropriate books that help to infer the meaning of the passages.

    Example
    I heard the sound of a vehicle drive up to my house, stop for a moment, and then drive away. I could hear the vehicle do the same thing at other houses on my block. I hoped my invitation for Justine's party had arrived.

    What is this passage about? *(The mail was being delivered.)*
    Which key words give you clues? *(vehicle, stop for a moment, drive away, hear the vehicle do the same thing at other houses, hoped my invitation had arrived)*

5. Make individuals aware of how to draw inferences between new information and the background knowledge from personal experiences they already have. Decide upon an idea or topic. Then select a passage(s) from age- or grade-appropriate books.

Between the Lines

Example

Idea: There are reasons why people cry.

Personal experience: Tell us something that might make you cry. *(pain, anger, sadness, fear, frustration)*

Passage: Tears streamed down Julia's cheeks as she tried to grab the scissors from her mother's hand. "I know how long your hair should be, Julia," said her mother. "You may think you look fine now, but wait until I'm finished. You'll see that I'm right."

After reading the passage, decide together which appears to be the most likely reason the girl cried.

6. Select several statements that concern feelings from textbooks. Read one aloud. Ask each individual to identify a feeling word for the statement, and write it on a piece of paper or a chalkboard. Each individual can then express another feeling word for that same statement, or move on to another statement. One rule: no feeling word which has already been written down can be repeated. More than one feeling can be expressed for each item. The use of a thesaurus should be encouraged.

    Next, ask each individual to choose one of the more unique feeling words from the previous activity and describe how he or she would typically express that feeling. Have students explain what they would look like and how they would behave.

7. Read a level-appropriate passage with students. Have students answer inferential questions and then select a title that will clarify the inferred material in a passage.

    Example

    It was a beautiful spring day. The sun was shining, and a strong wind was blowing from the east. Everyone running along the sand had a joyful expression on his or her face. They each had to be careful that their string didn't become entangled with the others'.

    Inferential questions:

    What are the people doing?
    Where do you think they are?
    Why are they running?
    What would cause the strings to become entangled?
    What is a good title for this passage?

Section 15: Bridging Activities

8. Have students listen to the beginning of a story and tell what they think will happen next.

   Example

   Shannon was told not to go into the pool until there was an adult around to watch her. She was very impatient and decided to go in anyway. Shannon…

9. Have students examine the comics section of the newspaper. Discuss the clues that help determine the basis of the humor of a comic strip or cartoon (see Section 13).

10. Collect brochures for well-known vacation areas. Read the description of activities, weather, accommodations, etc. Ask students to infer the location being advertised.

    Example

    Hike through lush rainforests, lounge on a secluded beach, cruise down a volcano on a mountain bike. You can snorkel, hike, explore, and enjoy a luau at sunset.
    (Location inference: *Hawaii*)

11. Read advertisements for various products from weekly flyers. Ask students to infer the product being advertised.

    Example

    Includes ice/water dispenser, top freezer, adjustable shelves, humidity control, crispers, and chilled meat-drawer.
    (Object inference: *refrigerator*)

12. Read introduction paragraphs of level-appropriate chapter books. Ask students to infer information about the setting (time and place of story).

13. Look at flyers from various stores (e.g., Wal-Mart). Have students categorize the items found on the individual pages

    Example

    On a page including radios, televisions, DVD players…
    (Category inference: *Electronics*)

14. Explore textbooks from students' classes. Find and discuss cause and effect relationships within the curriculum. For example, in history you could discuss the following:

Cause	Effect
Higher taxes	Boston Tea Party
Missiles in Cuba	Cuban Missile Crisis
Stock market crash	Great Depression

APPENDICES

Appendix A: Location Warm-Ups 149

Appendix B: Agent Warm-Ups 153

Appendix C: Time Warm-Ups 157

Appendix D: Action Warm-Ups 160

Appendix E: Instrument Warm-Ups 164

Appendix F: Category Warm-Ups 169

Appendix G: Object Warm-Ups 176

Appendix H: Feelings Warm-Ups 178

Appendix I: Cause and Effect Warm-Ups 179

Appendix J: Problem/Solution Warm-Ups 181

Appendix K: Paragraph Analysis Story Webs 183

Appendix A: Location Warm-Ups

Make It Clear Statements

1. The Bennett family was driving towards Grandma's house for Thanksgiving dinner. They only had to go two more miles before they got off the highway. Where was the Bennett family?

2. The bird sat on the bedroom windowsill. His early morning song woke Jake. Where was the bird?

3. Harriet hit the ball over the net with her tennis racquet. The ball landed, within bounds, on the other side of the court. Where was Harriet?

4. When the bell rang, the students packed up their books and left the classroom. Where were the students?

5. Howard stepped up to the plate and hit the ball out of the ballpark for a home run. Where was Howard?

6. Alice sat on one of the park swings. She watched Dick and Jane go up and down on the seesaw, and Jerry going down the slide. Where was Alice?

7. Tyrone jumped off the diving board and swam laps in the deep end of the pool for almost half an hour. Where was Tyrone?

8. Sonia selected three library books from the nonfiction section. She went to the librarian to check out the books. Sonia would have to return the books in two weeks. Where is Sonia?

9. Maurice took out the brushes and paint. He looked around his art studio and finally placed the easel where he could take best advantage of the morning light. He put on his smock before mixing paint on the palette. Where was Maurice?

10. The farmer and his family were busy picking apples from the trees in the orchard. They sold their apples every year. Where were the farmer and his family?

11. Mandy laced up her bowling shoes and took her bowling ball out of its bag. She started the game with two spares and a strike. She always has good luck at this bowling alley. Where was Mandy?

12. Jack climbed up to the top of the ladder that was leaning against the house, and stepped onto the roof. He pulled up the old, broken roofing tiles and put the new tiles in their place. Where was Jack?

Location Guesstimation Crossword

ACROSS

3. Jan needed to buy more cereal. After searching the shelf, she found the brand she liked. Jan was at the ___ store.
6. Randy had just had his appendix removed. When his friends came to visit him later that day, he showed them his scar. Randy was in the ___.
8. The mirror on the medicine cabinet was all fogged up when Juan finished taking a shower. Juan was in the ___.
9. Al got up, put on his slippers, and took his robe from the closet. He was very tired because he didn't sleep well. Al was in his ___.

DOWN

1. Milton looked up at the Eiffel Tower and marveled at its beauty. Milton was in ___.
2. Nora sat on the sand and built a sand castle at the water's edge. She was upset when a big wave came and washed away her castle. Nora was on the ___.
4. Frances tried on a dozen dresses before she found the one that fit just right. Now she had to walk down to the store that sold shoes to go with it. Frances is in the ___.
5. Naomi opened the refrigerator and took out the ingredients for a seafood salad. Naomi was in the ___.
7. The third act was about to begin. Lucy rushed back to her seat after the brief intermission. Lucy was in a ___.

Location Guesstimation Crossword Answer Key

Appendix A: Location Warm-Ups

Location Think Aloud Situations

1. Trevor entered the terminal and looked for the sign for the proper airline. He wheeled his luggage to the ticket counter and showed the agent his ticket and other identification. The agent put the luggage on a conveyor belt. Trevor went to the gate and took a seat. He had to wait for an hour. Where was Trevor?

2. Bianca took off her sandals and sat on the towel. She wiggled her toes in the sand and thought about going into the water. She decided to wait for Charlie to arrive so he could watch her belongings. Where was Bianca?

3. Every time Ryan approached a corner, the light turned red. At this rate, he thought he might be late for work. Fortunately, he made the left turn into the company parking lot at exactly 8:57 AM. Where was Ryan?

4. The surfboard was about 10 feet long. Eric stood up carefully and prepared to glide in on the next big wave. He had a feeling of exhilaration when he managed to stay on the board and ride the wave. Where was Eric?

5. Jake sharpened his pencil and waited for the math test to begin. He hoped he had studied enough. The teacher said the test would cover everything discussed in class during the past week. Where was Jake?

6. Claire found the repetitive sound the wheels made to be very soothing. The autumn scenery was especially pretty. She could see the tracks up ahead when she looked out of the window of the first car. The trip would be over in just one more hour. Where was Claire?

7. Evan placed his shoes and jeans in the locker and took out his tennis shoes and shorts. Today's game would determine if he could compete in the tennis club's semifinal event. When he looked up, his opponent was standing at his locker, smiling at him. Where was Evan?

8. Jennifer was snorkeling and enjoying the opportunity to see many colorful fish when she felt a hard blow to her foot. Another snorkeler had inadvertently kicked her with his flipper. Her foot hurt terribly. She had a hard time swimming back to shore. Where was Jennifer?

What Am I?

I hold a sign that says, "Stop." I stand at the corner of a school. I make sure children are safe when crossing the street.	I studied at a music conservatory. I listen to many children playing their violins. I give lessons that last about one-half hour.
I sit at a desk in a business office. I have to answer phones many times each day. I greet people as they come to the office for their appointments.	I am very good with numbers. I work long hours just before April 15th. I help people fill out their tax forms.
I stand when I do my job. I have to use many different hair products. I cut, dye, and perm hair.	I do my writing on a computer. I try to write at least five pages every day. I give my editor one new chapter each month.
I have to use a drill to do my job. I have an assistant who hands me instruments as I work. X-rays of teeth help me to determine what I must do.	I am very good at drawing. I can make pictures from verbal descriptions. I see my work in children's books.

What Am I?

I speak several different languages. I work at the United Nations. I listen to a speaker of one language and say his or her words to someone else in another language.	I work in a very quiet place. I make sure all materials are checked out with a date for their return. I help people find the books, videos, and magazines they want.
I drive a car. I help people in need. I arrest people when they break the law.	I drive a car. My job can be dangerous. I speed around a track.
I make people laugh. I wear colorful clothes. I wear a round, red nose.	I run a lot. I use a ball for my job. I like to make touchdowns.
I need to memorize a lot of material. I speak with a lot of expression. I have my hair and makeup done professionally.	I work in others' homes or businesses. I listen to how they want their spaces to look. I help them choose colors and decorations that would look nice.

Occupation Highlights

1. A doctor:
   a. Spends many years studying after leaving college
   b. Frequently has a stethoscope nearby
   c. Doesn't usually have patience for his or her patients

2. A musician:
   a. Generally practices many hours each day
   b. Has to audition each time he or she is going to play before an audience
   c. Only likes to associate with other musicians

3. A nurse:
   a. Prescribes medication for his or her patients
   b. Needs to be good in math
   c. Doesn't always wear white

4. A lawyer:
   a. Spends most of his or her time in the courtroom
   b. Has to have a license to practice
   c. Can defend or prosecute people

5. A ballerina:
   a. Practices dance steps for hours every day
   b. Usually practices in a pool
   c. Sometimes wears tutus when performing

6. A dog trainer:
   a. Uses treats to train dogs
   b. Has a way with animals
   c. Ignores dogs to get them to do tricks

7. A poet:
   a. Has to be sure the words in the poem rhyme
   b. Expresses ordinary thoughts in an imaginative and creative manner
   c. Often writes about love

8. A window washer:
   a. Should not be afraid of heights
   b. Uses a squeegee
   c. Always whistles while he or she is working

Appendix B: Agent Warm-Ups

9. A driving instructor:
   a. Should be a calm, even-tempered person
   b. Must know all the rules of the road
   c. Has to practice before going to work each day

10. An architect:
    a. Is exactly the same as an engineer
    b. Can advise people on how to construct a building
    c. Designs museums, cathedrals, hospitals, and many other buildings

11. A construction worker:
    a. Uses a variety of tools
    b. Needs to make careful measurements
    c. Designs new buildings

12. A house painter:
    a. Chooses his own paint colors
    b. Is often afraid of heights
    c. Uses a variety of brushes, rollers, and paint sprayers

13. A semitrailer truck driver:
    a. Is often away from home
    b. Often sleeps in his or her cab
    c. Always maintains healthy eating and sleeping habits

14. A custodian:
    a. Always works 9:00 AM to 5:00 PM
    b. Uses a variety of cleaning agents
    c. Uses a vacuum cleaner and a mop

15. A farmer:
    a. Grows a variety of crops
    b. Raises a variety of animals
    c. Always wears overalls

16. A pharmacist:
    a. Sells illegal drugs
    b. Needs to read a doctor's handwriting
    c. Fills patients' prescriptions

Appendix C: Time Warm-Ups

Beat the Clock

winter	New Year's Eve
January	Monday
spring	Mother's Day
March	Sunday

Between the Lines © 2006 C.C. Spector. Published by Thinking Publications.
Duplication permitted for educational use only.

Appendix C: Time Warm-Ups

Beat the Clock

summer	Fourth of July
June	Saturday
fall	Halloween
December	Thanksgiving

Name That Time

1. Arielle found it difficult to drive without her sunglasses because the sun was directly overhead. *(noon, midday)*

2. Susan had been reading a novel all afternoon. She flipped on the light switch so she could continue to read. *(dusk)*

3. Manuel dropped his school backpack on the chair in his room and ran outside to play. *(after school)*

4. Gregory's stomach was growling, and he felt very hungry. He was glad that his fourth period science class was almost over. *(lunchtime)*

5. After dinner, Sybil went to the movies. *(evening)*

6. Josephina could hardly wait for the day to be over. She was going to spend the weekend at a ski resort. *(Friday)*

7. Schlomo put his completed homework papers in his backpack and ran out the door to catch the bus. *(before school, morning)*

8. Rudy changed out of his tuxedo and Bess changed out of her gown. They had to catch a plane to Cancun, where they would spend their two-week honeymoon. *(after their wedding)*

9. Gideon swam, sailed, and enjoyed the beauty of the island. He had only three more days before he had to go back to work in the city. *(vacation time)*

10. Marilyn put out a clean towel and got the new bottle of shampoo. Now she was ready. *(before she washed her hair)*

11. Everything was packed up and ready for the moving men. This would be the last time the family would sleep in this house. *(the day before moving to a new location)*

12. Jared washed his hands, sat down, and put his napkin in his lap. *(before a meal)*

Appendix D: Action Warm-Ups

Gestures

kicking a football	waking up in the morning
catching a fly or other insect	describing a fish that was caught
skating on ice	rowing a boat
riding a bike	shaving a beard

Gestures

hailing a taxicab	reading a book
sweeping a floor	pumping gas at a gas station
flipping a pancake	unwrapping a candy bar
eating spaghetti	smelling a flower

Appendix D: Action Warm-Ups

What Am I Doing?

Isaac put on his underwear. He pulled his shirt over his head and put his arms into the sleeves. Then he put on his pants. Finally, he put on his socks and shoes.	Cynthia took the tarnished silver tray out of the closet. She spread the pieces out on the table. She found a soft clean rag. There was just enough silver polish left in the jar.
François took out a large bowl. He tore up the washed leaves and put them in the bowl. He chopped onions and mushrooms, and added them to the bowl. He shook the oil and vinegar in a jar until they were well blended.	Esther found a pattern. She bought fabric, thread, and buttons. She pinned the pattern pieces to the fabric. She cut each of the pieces carefully.
Jim filled the pitcher with water. He cut six lemons and squeezed them into the water. He added sugar. He stirred the mixture and put the pitcher into the refrigerator.	Ralph spread newspaper on the kitchen counter. He wiped his shoes with a cloth, and put them on the newspaper. He made sure he had a clean, dry buffing cloth. He took out the shoe polish.
Butch read the specials. He walked up to the counter. He gave his order. He carried his tray to the table.	Samantha arranged a bowl of fruit and put it on the table. She opened the shades so she would have lots of light. She put a canvas on an easel. She found her favorite box of watercolors, and her brushes.

What Am I Doing?

Jesse underlined several words in the book he was reading. He found his dictionary. He opened the dictionary and began his search. He started with the first word he had underlined.	Elmer woke up at 4:30 AM. He put on his clothes. He went to the barn. He picked up a pail and walked over to the cow.
Janice spread newspaper on the table. She got out a sharp knife. She drew a scary face. She cut the face design into the pumpkin.	Jerry went into the dressing room. He put on his suit. He rubbed sunscreen onto his body. He stuck his foot in the water to check its temperature.
Jake got out the large book. He looked up Dale's last name. He found the correct number. He pressed the corresponding numbers on the telephone.	Greg pushed the "on" button. He opened the jewel case. He pulled out the CD and placed it in. He turned up the volume and sang along.
Jean put on a helmet. She got out a saddle. She grabbed a bridle. She coaxed the horse to come by holding out an apple.	Kari got out the decorations. She put on the lights. She put the ornaments on. She finished up with some tinsel.

Tool Duel
Tools

ax	ax
shovel	shovel
brush	brush
spatula	spatula

Tool Duel
Tools

spoon	spoon
pliers	pliers
screwdriver	screwdriver
hammer	hammer

Appendix E: Instrument Warm-Ups

Tool Duel
Tasks

cut down a tree	split logs
eat soup	mix ingredients together
dig a hole	remove snow
pull out nails	loosen screws

Tool Duel
Tasks

paint walls	groom one's hair
turn a screw	pry something up
flip pancakes	serve cake
pound in a nail	remove a nail

Appendix E: Instrument Warm-Ups

Tool Addition

1. Corey trimmed his toenails with...
2. Amanda curled her hair with...
3. Warren wrote the letter with...
4. Gretchen ate with...
5. Douglas dug holes for his bulbs with...
6. Annette played the tune on...
7. Dennis held the papers together with...
8. Maryanne locked the door with...
9. Sam told time with...
10. Colita cleaned the floor with...
11. Isaiah finished his art project with...
12. Jordan hung the poster with...
13. Colin made a colorful drawing with...
14. Katrina measured the wall with...
15. Julia tightened the nut with...
16. Elysia scraped the bowl with...
17. Mioko calculated the math problems with...
18. Marcus hung the picture with...
19. Dominic measured the ingredients with...
20. Kayla recorded the song with...

Appendix F: Category Warm-Ups

Category Stack-Up Race
Category Names

Objects That Cut	Objects Worn around the Neck
Wind Instruments	Bodies of Water

Between the Lines © 2006 C.C. Spector. Published by Thinking Publications.
Duplication permitted for educational use only.

Appendix F: Category Warm-Ups

Category Stack-Up Race
Category Names

Stringed Instruments	Objects Worn on the Feet
Types of Movies	Objects Found in or on a Desk

Category Stack-Up Race
Category Members

knife	necklace
flute	ocean
violin	boots
comedy	stapler

Category Stack-Up Race
Category Members

saw	scarf
clarinet	river
cello	slippers
horror	paper clips

Category Stack-Up Race
Category Members

razor	collar
saxophone	creek
guitar	socks
animated	notepad

Appendix F: Category Warm-Ups

Class Classification

Instruments	Flowers
Pizza Toppings	Snack Foods
Chairs	Appliances
Trees	Vehicles

Class Classification

Means of Communication	Beverages
Types of Music	Objects to Tell Time
Shades of Blue	Party Decorations
Savannah Animals	Clothing Articles

Appendix G: Object Warm-Ups

Twenty Questions

Pet (turtle)	Something That Grows (hair)
Winter Clothing (scarf)	Vehicle (motorcycle)
Dessert (brownie)	Game (Ping Pong)
Insect (butterfly)	Beverage (lemonade)

Appendix G: Object Warm-Ups

Twenty Questions

Forest Animal (skunk)	Breakfast Food (cereal)
Instrument (piano)	Something You Read (poetry)
Body of Water (lake)	Information Source (Internet)
Clothing (skirt)	Jewelry (bracelet)

Appendix H: Feelings Warm-Ups

Expressions

Afraid	Annoyed
Enraged	Surprised
Angry	Guilty
Worried	Impatient

Appendix I: Cause and Effect Warm-Ups

Why?

1. Tim and Maureen O'Brian rushed to the hospital. Why?
2. Jack arrived at school with wet sneakers. Why?
3. Jessie looked at Whit and started to laugh. Why?
4. Unexpectedly, Herb had to drive to the supermarket. Why?
5. Toby glared at Carla when she entered the room. Why?
6. Lester fell down the stairs. Why?
7. Chloe was driving along Route 66 when she stopped her car. Why?
8. Samantha walked away from the table without eating her dinner. Why?
9. Sparky got up and turned off the TV. Why?
10. Kyle came home from the fair feeling ill. Why?
11. Sheila had a look of horror on her face. Why?
12. Kazuko spent the entire day cooking. Why?
13. Mel didn't want to drive all the way to the city. Why?
14. Nina was very unhappy about her vacation. Why?
15. Russell experienced a feeling of wonder. Why?
16. Winston ran as fast as he could. Why?
17. Tou looked in her son's room with disappointment. Why?
18. Shannon was up all night. Why?
19. Daniel climbed up to the roof. Why?
20. Alan ended up with a dirty shirt. Why?

Appendix 1: Cause and Effect Warm-Ups

And On and On and On...
What could happen if someone...

1. Drove past their exit on the parkway?
2. Won the lottery?
3. Ate too much dinner?
4. Forgot to put the lock on their locker?
5. Came home after their curfew?
6. Got to school and realized they left their homework on the kitchen table?
7. Had an argument with their best friend?
8. Forgot to wear their bike helmet?
9. Finally learned how to ice-skate?
10. Wanted to see a horror film but their friend wanted to see a comedy?
11. Spilled chocolate milk all over the table?
12. Frequently complimented people?
13. Forgot to water their garden?
14. Found $20.00 on the sidewalk?
15. Played jokes on their friends?
16. Parked illegally near a fire hydrant?
17. Lost their wallet?
18. Forgot to let the cat in at night?
19. Sent a surprise bouquet of birthday balloons to a friend's workplace?
20. Won tickets to a popular concert?

Appendix J: Problem/Solution Warm-Ups

Problem/Solution Think Aloud Situations

1. My parents just told me that they are getting a divorce. My mom and dad both want me to live with them. They said it is my choice. I don't know what to do.

2. My best friend wants me to take art class with her next year. She was in art this year and says the teacher is really nice. I'm not interested in art. I was planning on taking choir instead.

3. All of my friends are going to the dance on Friday. They all decided to buy dresses at the same store that are similar in style, but different colors. The dresses cost $200 each. I can't afford the dress.

4. I really want a dog. My parents say I can't have a dog because I wouldn't take care of it. I have been around my friends' dogs a lot, and I know I would be good with one of my own. I don't know how to convince them to let me get a dog.

5. I have three tests on Thursday. I really want to do well in all of my classes, but I just don't know how I can study for all three tests on the same day.

6. My best friend is wearing a lot of makeup lately. She thinks it looks really good. Everyone at school is talking about her behind her back, saying that her new look is unattractive. I think she needs to know the truth, but I don't want to hurt her feelings.

7. My best friend and I have been on the football team together since elementary school. This year we had try outs, and he didn't make the team. He wants me to quit the team because he thinks the coach was being unfair. I want to be loyal to my friend, but I still want to play football.

Appendix J: Problem/Solution Warm-Ups

Help Is on the Way

1. What would you do if you realized you were still wearing your bedroom slippers when you got to school?

2. What would you do if you accidentally damaged a library book?

3. What would you do if you went to the refreshment stand for ice cream while at the beach, and you couldn't find your way back to where your family was sitting?

4. What would you do if you arrived at a party and someone else was wearing the same outfit you had on?

5. What would you do if you were sitting in class taking a test and your nose started to bleed?

6. What would you do if you found out that your best friend told another person something about you that was supposed to be kept secret?

7. What would you do if you wanted your room painted green and your mom wanted it to be painted a different color?

8. What would you do if you saw someone put a dent into a parked car and then drive away?

9. What would you do if a friend dared you to eat a worm?

10. What would you do if you were out sailing on a lake and you saw someone fall overboard?

11. What would you do if you saw a bunch of bullies beating up a little boy?

12. What would you do if you were invited to a friend's house for dinner and she served something you absolutely hated?

Paragraph Analysis Story Web
Example

Topic Sentence:
Lee was dedicated to her ice skating practice.

Related Sentence:
She practiced figure eights and quick turns for five hours before leaving the ice.

Related Sentence:
Spins were on her agenda for the next day.

Related Sentence:
If she continued to practice every day, she would have a good chance at winning the gold medal.

New Sentence:
She was very systematic in her efforts to reach her goal.

This Sentence Does Not Belong:
Her outfit was blue and white.

Appendix K: Paragraph Analysis Story Webs

Paragraph Analysis Story Web

Topic Sentence:

↓

Related Sentence:

↓

Related Sentence:

↓

Related Sentence:

↓

New Sentence:

This Sentence Does Not Belong:

References

Ackerman, B. P. (1986). Referential and causal coherence in the story comprehension of children and adults. *Journal of Experimental Child Psychology, 41,* 336–366.

Bass, G. M., Jr., & Perkins, H. W. (1984). Teaching critical thinking skills with CAI. *Electronic Learning, 14*(2), 32, 34, 96.

Baum, R. (1990). Finishing touches—10 top programs. *Learning, 18*(6), 51–55.

Bloom, B. S., Engelhart, M. D., Furst, E. J., Hill, W. H., & Krathwohl, D. R. (1956). *Taxonomy of educational objectives: The classification of educational goals. Handbook 1: Cognitive domain.* New York: David McKay.

Bloom, L., & Lahey, M. (1978). *Language development and language disorders.* New York: John Wiley.

Bransford, J. D., Burns, M. S., Delclos, V. R., & Vye, N. J. (1986). Teaching thinking: Evaluating evaluations and broadening the data base. *Educational Leadership, 44*(2), 68–70.

Buehl, D. (2001). *Inferences: Learning how to make them.* Wisconsin Literacy Education and Reading Network Source (WILEARNS). Retrieved November 5, 2004, from http://wilearns.state.wi.us/apps/Print.asp?ap=&cid=135

Carrow-Woolfolk, E. (1988). *Theory, assessment and intervention in language disorders: An integrative approach.* Orlando, FL: Grune and Stratton.

Case, R. (1985). *Intellectual development: Birth to adulthood.* Orlando, FL: Academic Press.

Cotton, K. (1988). *Classroom questioning: Close-up No. 5.* Portland, OR: Northwest Regional Educational Laboratory. Retrieved February 18, 2004, from http://www.nwrel.org/scpd/sirs/6/cu11.html

Cotton, K. (2001). *Teaching thinking skills.* Retrieved November 2, 2004, from http://www.nwrel.org/scpd/sirs/6/cu11.html

Crais, E., & Chapman, R. (1987). Story recall and inferencing skills in language/learning disabled and nondisabled children. *Journal of Speech and Hearing Disorders, 52,* 50–55.

Crump, W. D., Schlichter, C. L., & Palk, B. E. (1988). Teaching HOTS in the middle and high school: A district-level initiative in developing higher order thinking skills. *Roeper Review, 10*(4), 205–211.

Doran, J., & Anderson, A. (2003). Inferencing skills of adolescent readers who are hearing impaired. *Journal of Research in Reading, 26,* 256–266.

Edwards, A. L. (1973). *Statistical methods* (3rd ed.). New York: Holt, Rinehart and Winston.

Fischer, K., & Pipp, S. (1984). Processes of cognitive development: Optimal level and skill acquisition. In R. Sternberg (Ed.), *Mechanisms of cognitive development* (pp. 45–81). New York: Freeman.

Flavell, J. H., & Wellman, H. M. (1980). Metamemory. In R. V. Kail & J. W. Hagen (Eds.), *Memory in cognitive development* (pp. 3–33). Hillsdale, NJ: Erlbaum.

Gough, D. (1991). *Thinking about thinking.* Alexandria, VA: National Association of Elementary School Principals.

Haller, E. P., Child, D. A., & Walberg, H. J. (1988). Can comprehension be taught? A quantitative synthesis of 'metacognitive' studies. *Educational Researcher, 17*(9), 5–8.

Herrnstein, R. J., Nickerson, R. S., de Sanchez, M., & Swets, J. A. (1986). Teaching thinking skills. *American Psychologist, 41,* 1279–1289.

Honeck, R. P., Voegtle, K., Dorfmueller, M. A., & Hoffman, R. R. (1980). Proverbs, meaning, and group structure. In R. P. Honeck & R. R. Hoffman (Eds.), *Cognition and figurative language* (pp. 127–161). Hillsdale, NJ: Erlbaum.

Hudgins, B., & Edelman, S. (1986). Teaching critical thinking skills to fourth and fifth graders through teacher-led small-group discussions. *Journal of Educational Research, 79*(6), 333–342.

Isen, A. M., Daubman, K. A., & Nowicki, G. P. (1987). Positive affect facilitates creative problem solving. *Journal of Personality and Social Psychology, 52,* 1122–1131.

Johnson, D. D., & von Hoff Johnson, B. (1986). Highlighting vocabulary in inferential comprehension. *Journal of Reading, 29,* 622–625.

Kagan, D. M. (1988). Evaluating a language arts program designed to teach higher level thinking skills. *Reading Improvement, 25*(1), 29–33.

Kamhi, A. G. (1987). Metalinguistic abilities in language-impaired children. *Topics in Language Disorders, 7*(2), 1–12.

Karmiloff-Smith, A. (1979). *A functional approach to child language.* Cambridge, UK: Cambridge University Press.

Klein, H. B., & Moses, N. (1994). *Intervention planning for children with communication disorders.* Englewood Cliffs, NJ: Prentice Hall.

Klein-Konigsberg, E. (1984). Semantic integration and language learning disabilities: From research to assessment and intervention. In G. P. Wallach & K. G. Butler (Eds.), *Language learning disabilities in school-age children* (pp. 251–270). Baltimore, MD: Williams and Wilkins.

Laing, S. P., & Kamhi, A. G. (2002). The use of think-aloud protocols to compare inferencing abilities in average and below-average readers. *Journal of Learning Disabilities, 35*(5), 436–447.

Larson, V. L., & McKinley, N. L. (2003). *Communication solutions for older students: Assessment and intervention strategies.* Greenville, SC: Thinking Publications University.

Lazzari, A. M., & Peters, P. M. (1988). *HELP 3: Handbook of exercises for language processing.* Moline, IL: LinguiSystems.

Lidz, C. S. (1991). *Practitioner's guide to dynamic assessment.* New York: Guilford.

Makkai, A., Boatner, M. T., & Gates, J. E. (1995). *A dictionary of American idioms.* New York: Barron's Educational Series.

Matthews, D. B. (1989). The effect of a thinking-skills program on the cognitive abilities of middle school students. *Clearing House, 62*(5), 202–204.

Mid-Continent Research for Education and Learning (McREL; 2000). *A compilation of content standards for K–12 curriculum.* Retrieved February 12, 2005, from www.mcrel.org/standards-benchmarks

Myers, P. S. (1986). Right hemisphere communication impairment. In R. Chapey (Ed.), *Language intervention strategies in adult aphasia* (pp. 444–461). Baltimore: Williams and Wilkins.

Nelson, N. W. (1993). *Childhood language disorders in context: Infancy through adolescence.* New York: Macmillan.

Nippold, M. A., Allen, M. M., & Kirsch, D. I. (2001). Proverb comprehension as a function of reading proficiency in preadolescents. *Language, Speech, and Hearing Services in Schools, 32,* 90–100.

Pearson, P. D. (1982). *A context for instructional research on reading comprehension.* Cambridge, MA: Bolt, Beranek and Newman.

Piaget, J. (1985). *The equilibration of cognitive structures: The central problem of intellectual development.* Chicago: University of Chicago Press.

Pinker, S. (1990). Language acquisition. In D. N. Osherson & H. Lasnik (Eds.), *An invitation to cognitive science* (pp. 197–241). Cambridge, MA: Massachusetts Institute of Technology Press.

Pinker, S. (1991). *Learnability and cognition.* Cambridge, MA: Massachusetts Institute of Technology Press.

Pogrow, S. (1988). HOTS: A thinking skills program for at risk students. *Principal, 67*(4), 19–24.

Reid, D. K. (1988). *Teaching the learning disabled: A cognitive developmental approach.* Needham, MA: Allyn & Bacon.

Schneider, P., & Watkins, R. V. (1996). Applying Vygotskian developmental theory to language intervention. *Language, Speech, and Hearing Services in Schools, 27*(2), 157–170.

Simon, C. S. (1993). *300$^+$ developmental language strategies for clinic and classroom.* Tempe, AZ: Communi-Cog Publications.

Simpson, J. (1996). *The concise Oxford dictionary of proverbs.* New York: Oxford University Press.

Spears, R. A. (1996). *NTC's American idioms dictionary.* Lincolnwood, IL: National Textbook Company.

Spector, C. C. (1990). Linguistic humor comprehension of normal and language-impaired adolescents. *Journal of Speech and Hearing Disorders, 55,* 533–541.

Spector, C. C. (1997). *Saying one thing, meaning another: Activities for clarifying ambiguous language.* Greenville, SC: Super Duper Publications.

Spector, C. C. (2002). *As far as words go: Unraveling the complexities of ambiguous language and humor.* Greenville, SC: Super Duper Publications.

Spector, C. C. (2005, April). *Inferencing skills of university students for visual humor items.* Poster session presented at the annual convention of the New York State Speech-Language-Hearing Association, Huntington, NY.

Sternberg, R. G., & Bhana, K. (1986). Synthesis of research on the effectiveness of intellectual skills programs: Snake-oil remedies or miracle cures? *Educational Leadership, 44*(2), 60–67.

van Kleeck, A. (1984). Metalinguistic skills: Cutting across spoken and written language and problem-solving abilities. In G. Wallach & K. Butler (Eds.), *Language learning disabilities in school-age children* (pp.128–153). Baltimore: Williams and Wilkins.

van Kleeck, A., & Richardson, A. (1986). What's in an error? Wrong responses as language teaching opportunities. *NSSLHA Journal, 14,* 25–50.

Vygotsky, L. S. (1962). *Thought and language.* Cambridge, MA: Massachusetts Institute of Technology Press.

Wallach, G. P., & Lee, A. D. (1982). So you want to know what to do with language-disabled children above the age of six. In K. G. Butler & G. P. Wallach (Eds.), *Language disorders and learning disabilities* (pp. 99–113). Rockville, MD: Aspen.

Wallach, G. P., & Lee-Schachter, A. D. (1984). *Language activities for learning disabled students.* Boston, MA: The Scarborough Board of Education.

Wallach, G. P., & Miller, L. (1988). *Language intervention and academic success.* Boston: College-Hill.

Wechsler, D. (1997). *Wechsler Adult Intelligence Scales–3rd Edition (WAIS–III).* San Antonio, TX: The Psychological Corporation.

Wechsler, D. (2003). *Wechsler Intelligence Scales for Children–4th Edition (WISC–IV).* San Antonio, TX: The Psychological Corporation.

Westby, C. (1984). Development of narrative language abilities. In G. P. Wallach & K. G. Butler (Eds.), *Language learning disabilities in school-age children* (pp. 103–127). Baltimore, MD: Williams and Wilkins.

Whimbey, A. (1985). Test results from teaching thinking. In A. L. Costa (Ed.), *Developing minds: A resource book* for teaching thinking (pp. 269–271). Alexandria, VA: Association for Supervision and Curriculum Development.

Wiig, E. H., & Secord, W. (1989). *Test of Language Competence–Expanded Edition (TLC–E).* San Antonio, TX: The Psychological Corporation.

Wiig, E. H., & Wiig, K. M. (1999). *On conceptual learning.* Retrieved August 22, 2001, from http://www.krii.com/articles.htm

Ziv, A. (1988). Humor as a social corrective. In L. Behrens & L. J. Rosen (Eds.), *Writing and reading across the curriculum* (3rd ed.; pp. 356–360). Glenview, IL: Scott, Foresman and Company.

iris
INTEGRATED REFUGEE
& IMMIGRANT SERVICES

Thank you for joining us for the screening of SOUFRA!

And thank you as well for purchasing a SOUFRA Cookbook.

Proceeds from the sale of this cookbook will benefit the children's center being developed by the women in the film and it will help refugees being resettled in Connecticut, through IRIS.

The value of goods you received with this cookbook is $20, with the remainder being tax-deductible to the extent allowed by law, through IRIS (tax ID 06-0653044).

235 Nicoll Street | Second Floor | New Haven, CT 06511
TELEPHONE: (203) 562-2095 | FAX: (203) 562-1798 | EMAIL: info@irisct.org | WEB: irisct.org